The Southeast

The
Southeast

GREENWOOD PRESS
Westport, Connecticut • London

Library of Congress Cataloging-in-Publication Data

Creative Media Applications
    How geography affects the United States/Creative Media Applications.
    p. cm.
    Summary: Explores the ways in which geography has affected the lives of the people of the United States.
    Includes bibliographical references (p.).
    Contents: v.1. Northeast — v.2. Southeast — v.3. Midwest — v.4. West — v.5. Southwest.
    ISBN 0-313-32250-3 (set) — 0-313-32251-1 (Northeast) — 0-313-32252-X (Southeast) — 0-313-32253-8 (Midwest) — 0-313-32254-6 (West) — 0-313-32255-4 (Southwest)
    1. United States — Geography — Juvenile literature. 2. Human geography — United States — Juvenile literature. 3. United States — History, Local — Juvenile literature. 4. Regionalism — United States — Juvenile literature. [1. United States — Geography.] I. Creative Media Applications.

E161.3.H69 2002
304.2'0973—dc21
    2002075304

British Library Cataloguing in Publication Data is available.

Library of Congress Catalog Card Number: 2002075304
ISBN: 0-313-32250-3   (set)
          0-313-32251-1   (Northeast)
          0-313-32252-X   (Southeast)
          0-313-32253-8   (Midwest)
          0-313-32254-6   (West)
          0-313-32255-4   (Southwest)

First published in 2002

Greenwood Press, 88 Post Road West, Westport, CT 06881
An imprint of Greenwood Publishing Group, Inc.
www.greenwood.com

Printed in the United States of America

The paper used in this book complies with the Permanent Paper Standard issued by the National Information Standards Organization (Z39.48–1984).

10 9 8 7 6 5 4 3 2 1

A Creative Media Applications, Inc. Production
Writer: Robin Doak
Design and Production: Fabia Wargin Design, Inc.
Editor: Matt Levine
Copyeditor: Laurie Lieb
Proofreader: Tania Bissell
AP Photo Researcher: Yvette Reyes
Consultant: Dean M. Hanink, Department of Geography,
    University of Connecticut
Maps: Ortelius Design

Photo Credits:
Cover: ©Photodisc, Inc.
AP/Wide World Photographs *pages:* ix, 4, 14, 34, 42, 47, 48, 50, 55, 57, 59, 61, 65, 67, 72, 74, 75, 76, 83, 87, 89, 99, 103, 105, 121, 123, 124
©CORBIS *pages:* 22, 28, 126
©Bettmann/CORBIS *pages:* 10, 95, 109, 113
Archiving Early America *page:* 7
©Buddy May/CORBIS *page:* 111
©William A Bake /CORBIS *page:* 114
©Lake County Museum /CORBIS *page:* 115

Contents

Introduction

The Southeast region of the United States is bordered by the Atlantic Ocean to the east, the Gulf of Mexico to the south, the Southwest region to the west, and the Northeast and Midwest regions to the north. There are twelve states in the Southeast: Alabama, Arkansas, Florida, Georgia, Kentucky, Louisiana, Mississippi, North Carolina, South Carolina, Tennessee, Virginia, and West Virginia.

The Southeast has a variety of landforms, from heavily forested mountain areas to white, sandy beaches along the Atlantic and gulf coasts. In the early days of settlement, both the mountain and coastal areas played important roles in the region's quickly growing economy. Fertile farmlands at the base of such mountains as the Appalachians and the Ouachitas encouraged settlement and expansion. The coast proved to be a benefit for shipping and trade.

The climate of the Southeast ranges from temperate in the northernmost states to semitropical along the southern reaches. In Florida and other southerly points, winter temperatures rarely fall below freezing. Long, hot summers and warm autumns and springs have attracted residents and visitors alike to the area.

The Southeast
Makes a Comeback

The first people to settle along the Atlantic coast in the Southeast were ancestors of later Native American tribes. Thousands of years ago, these people had traveled across a "land bridge" that connected Asia to North America. Descendants of these first arrivals included Algonquian-speaking tribes (Algonquins, Powhatans, Secotans) and Muskogean-speaking people (Creeks, Chickasaw, Choctaw). Other tribes in the area were the Cherokee (CHAYR-uh-key), Catawba, Natchez, and Calusa.

Some of the earliest European settlements in the United States were located in the Southeast. The Spanish were the first to arrive. They explored Florida in 1513 and founded St. Augustine (San Augustín) in 1565. St. Augustine was the first permanent European settlement in the United States.

Although the Spanish were the first, the English had the greatest impact in the Southeast. The first permanent English settlement, James Towne (later Jamestown), Virginia, was founded in 1607. More English settlements followed, and soon the English controlled most of the Southeast from Virginia to Georgia.

The French also played an important part in the early settlement of the Southeast. They explored the Mississippi River and founded colonies in Louisiana, Alabama, and Mississippi. Biloxi in Mississippi and Baton Rouge and New Orleans in Louisiana all started as French settlements.

One important event had a profound effect on the Southeast: the Civil War (1861–1865) between the North and the South. During those four years, thousands of troops in the Southeast region battled to preserve states' rights, the plantation system, and slavery. By the end of the struggle, the Southeast had been devastated. It would take more than half a century to restore the region's prosperity.

Since the Civil War, the Southeast has seen many changes. During the 1960s, the civil rights movement helped bring an end to the segregation of blacks and whites in the region. *Segregation* is the practice of separating one group of people from another. In recent years, the region has been recognized as ideal for economic growth and opportunities. It has attracted many new industries and residents with its mild climate and lower cost of living. Tourism is important, too—millions of tourists visit the Southeast each year to enjoy its breathtaking scenery and southern hospitality.

Children play on Panama City Beach in between bands of evening showers as the Gulf of Mexico churns and Tropical Storm Barry heads toward the Florida Panhandle, Sunday, Aug. 5, 2001, in Panama City Beach, Fla.

STATE BIRTHDAYS

Two of the earliest settlements in the nation were founded in the Southeast—Saint Augustine, Florida; and Jamestown, Virginia.

State	Capital	First Permanent European Settlement	Date of Statehood	Order of Statehood
Alabama	Montgomery	Mobile, 1702	December 14, 1819	22
Arkansas	Little Rock	Arkansas Post, 1686	June 15, 1836	25
Florida	Tallahassee	St. Augustine, 1567	March 3, 1845	27
Georgia	Atlanta	Savannah, 1733	January 2, 1788	4
Kentucky	Frankfort	Harrodsborough, 1774	June 1, 1792	15
Louisiana	Baton Rouge	Natchitoches, 1714	April 30, 1812	18
Mississippi	Jackson	Fort Maurepas, 1699	December 10, 1817	20
North Carolina	Raleigh	Edenton, c. 1658	November 21, 1789	12
South Carolina	Columbia	Charles Towne, 1670	May 23, 1788	8
Tennessee	Nashville	Watauga Valley, 1769	June 1, 1796	16
Virginia	Richmond	James Towne, 1607	June 25, 1788	10
West Virginia	Charleston	Sheperdstown, 1732	June 20, 1863	35

MORE STATE STATS

The largest state in the Southeast is Georgia, with nearly 58,000 square miles of land. The smallest is West Virginia. Here, the Southeast states are ordered from smallest to largest.

State	Size of Land Area	Size Rank	Population	Pop. Rank
West Virginia	24,087 square miles (62,626 square kilometers)	41	1,808,300	37
South Carolina	30,111 square miles (78,289 square kilometers)	40	4,012,000	26
Virginia	39,598 square miles (102,955 square kilometers)	37	7,078,500	12
Kentucky	39,732 square miles (103,303 square kilometers)	36	4,041,700	25
Tennessee	41,220 square miles (107,172 square kilometers)	34	5,689,200	16
Louisiana	43,566 square miles (113,272 square kilometers)	33	4,468,900	22
Mississippi	46,914 square miles (121,976 square kilometers)	31	2,844,600	31
North Carolina	48,718 square miles (126,667 square kilometers)	29	8,049,300	11
Alabama	50,750 square miles (131,950 square kilometers)	28	4,447,100	23
Arkansas	52,075 square miles (135,395 square kilometers)	27	2,673,400	33
Florida	53,997 square miles (140,392 square kilometers)	26	15,982,300	4
Georgia	57,919 square miles (150,589 square kilometers)	21	8,186,400	10

NOTE: All metric conversions in this book are approximate.

Appalachian Mountains

1

The Appalachian Mountains are the second-largest mountain system in the United States. Only the Rocky Mountains are larger. The Appalachians stretch more than 1,600 miles (2,560 kilometers) throughout the eastern United States. They parallel the Atlantic coast from central Alabama all the way to Newfoundland, Canada. In the Southeast, the Appalachians pass through Virginia, West Virginia, Kentucky, Tennessee, North Carolina, Georgia, and Alabama.

Geologists believe that the Appalachians are the oldest mountain system in North America. Parts of the Appalachians are twice as old as the Rocky Mountains. They began forming about 450 million years ago. The building process continued until about 250 million years ago. Over the centuries, wind and water wore down the high, jagged peaks of the mountains. Unlike the northern Appalachians, the southern Appalachians were not affected by glaciers. For this reason, the peaks in the south are higher and less rounded than those in the north. There is also more plant and animal diversity in the southern Appalachians.

The Appalachians are made up of several distinct mountain ranges. In the Southeast, these ranges include the Cumberland, Blue Ridge, Great Smoky, and Allegheny Mountains. Ridges and valleys mark the land around the ranges. The Tennessee, Shenandoah, Virginia, and Great Valleys are areas of fertile farmland that are flatter and more populated than the mountainous regions themselves.

Plateaus are another important geographic feature of the Appalachian region. *Plateaus* are elevated areas of land that are either flat or gently sloping. Some of the key plateaus in the southern Appalachians include the Piedmont, Cumberland, and Dahlonega

• *Fast Fact* •

At 6,684 feet (2,005 meters) high, Mount Mitchell, in the Black Mountains of North Carolina, is the tallest mountain east of the Mississippi River.

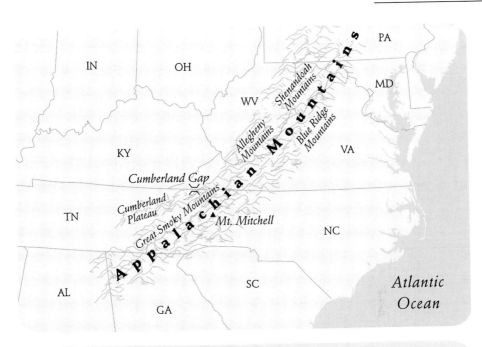

MOUNTAIN RANGES OF
THE SOUTHEASTERN APPALACHIANS

The Appalachians can be divided into several distinct ranges. The easternmost range, the Blue Ridge Mountains, is the backbone of the entire system. The mountain groups in the Southeast are as follows.

Range	States	Highest Mountain and Elevation
Cumberland Mountains	Alabama, Georgia, Tennessee, Kentucky, Virginia, West Virginia	Big Black Mountain, Kentucky: 4,145 feet (1,244 meters)
Great Smoky Mountains	North Carolina, Tennessee	Clingmans Dome, Tennessee: 6,643 feet (1,993 meters)
Blue Ridge Mountains/ Black Mountains	Georgia, North Carolina, Virginia, West Virginia	Mount Mitchell, North Carolina: 6,684 feet (2,005 meters)
Allegheny Mountains	Virginia, West Virginia, *Maryland, *Pennsylvania	Spruce Knob, West Virginia: 4,860 feet (1,458 meters)

* Not Southeastern states

Plateaus. The Piedmont Plateau is the easternmost plateau of the Appalachian system, while the Cumberland Plateau covers the southwestern part of the region.

SETTLING BY THE FALL LINE

The Piedmont Plateau is separated from the Atlantic coastal plain by the "fall line." The fall line is a place in the Appalachians where waterfalls and rapids occur in streams and rivers, which made it difficult for colonial boats to travel any further upstream. For this reason, many cities developed along the fall line, including Richmond, Virginia; Raleigh, North Carolina; and Augusta, Georgia.

Settlement in the Appalachians

The first people to settle in the southern Appalachians were the ancestors of later Native American groups. These early arrivals came to the mountain area about 10,000 years ago. Thousands of years later, many tribes made their homes in this area. These groups included the Choctaw, Chickasaw, Shawnee, Creek, and Mingo. The largest tribe in the area was the Cherokee (CHAYR-uh-key). Like other Appalachian tribes, the Cherokee hunted, fished, and grew crops of corn, beans, and squash. Before the first Europeans arrived in North America, there may have been as many as 50,000 Cherokee living in an area that included parts of eight states.

• Fast Fact •

Hernando de Soto named the Appalachians after a Native American tribe in northern Florida: the Apalachee.

In 1540, Spanish explorer Hernando de Soto made his way from Florida into the southern Appalachians. In his quest for gold, de Soto cruelly mistreated the Native Americans he met. He raided native villages, kidnapping, torturing, and murdering along the way. Two years later, de Soto died in the New World, having found neither gold nor glory. He and his soldiers left behind European diseases that would wipe out large numbers of the native populations throughout the Southeast. One of these disease may have been the deadly smallpox.

European Colonization

Until the mid-1700s, the Appalachians acted as a natural barrier to western settlement. As more and more colonists arrived in America, however, the best land along the Atlantic coast was quickly claimed. New arrivals from Europe began looking for ways to breach the high peaks in order to find their own lands to settle beyond the mountains.

The first path through the Appalachians used by settlers in the Southeast went through a notch in the hills where Kentucky, Tennessee, and Virginia meet: the Cumberland Gap. This narrow, winding footpath was first used by Native American hunting and war parties. In 1750, a group led by Dr. Thomas Walker located the gap, and the rush to the west was on.

The Cumberland Gap quickly became a major roadway for people traveling west. The first settlers to use the trail were English, Scotch-Irish, and German pioneers. These settlers made their homes in the valleys and flatlands at the foot of the mountains. Later settlers moved into the rugged mountains, determined to make better lives for themselves than the ones they had left behind in Europe.

Despite the opening of the Cumberland Gap, transportation into and out of the mountains remained difficult for most people. Those who settled in the Appalachians found that they were cut off from the rest of the colonies. To survive, they had to fend for themselves. These early mountain dwellers built log cabins using timber from the surrounding forests. They ate chicken, as well as corn and other vegetables they raised. They hunted deer in the woods and fished in streams and springs. The Appalachian settlers quickly earned a reputation for strength and independence.

Even into the twentieth century, life continued to be hard for many people living in the Appalachians. Inadequate roadways and poor transportation limited access to good medical and educational services. In the 1930s, poverty in parts of the Southeastern Appalachians, sometimes called *Appalachia*, became a serious regional problem.

DANIEL BOONE, TRAILBLAZER

One of the most famous people to travel through the Cumberland Gap was frontiersman Daniel Boone. In 1775, Boone and a group of settlers blazed the Wilderness Road, a wagon trail that passed from Virginia through the Cumberland Gap to the fertile Kentucky bluegrass region. After crossing the Appalachians, Boone established the town of Boonesborough, Kentucky. Boone and his group opened up the land west of the Appalachians for tens of thousands of settlers from the east.

The Cherokee Nation

In the mid-1700s, the ever-increasing number of settlers in the Appalachian area resulted in friction between the colonists and the Cherokee (CHAYR-uh-key). In an effort to stop colonists from taking their land, the Cherokee and other tribes often attacked and raided colonial settlements.

The Cherokee War (1759–1761) began when a group of colonists from Virginia killed and scalped more than twenty Cherokee. To prevent revenge by the tribe, colonial troops marched into Cherokee villages. They destroyed fields, burned homes, and took Cherokee land. The Cherokee retaliated, attacking settlements and killing colonists when they had the chance.

In 1761, the Cherokee surrendered. They signed a treaty that gave the colonists control of the eastern Cherokee lands in North and South Carolina. During the next few decades, the Cherokee agreed to more than twenty treaties with the Americans in attempts to maintain parts of their homeland.

During the American Revolution (1775–1783), the Cherokee supported the British in their fight with the colonists. By taking up arms against the colonists, Native American tribes hoped to stop any further settlement of their land. British officers encouraged the Cherokee and other tribes to attack Appalachian settlements. One British general went so far as to pay Native Americans for each settler's scalp collected. After the war, the Cherokee would pay dearly for their assistance to the British.

In 1828, gold was discovered on Cherokee land in Dahlonega, Georgia. The first major U.S. gold rush was on. The beginning of gold prospecting in Dahlonega marked the end for the Cherokee in the Appalachians. Gold miners and settlers demanded that the Cherokee be removed from the area.

NATIVE AMERICAN PLACE NAMES

Groups such as the Cherokee were driven out of the Appalachians, but Native American place names remain today.

Allegheny—"great warpath"

Kentucky—"dark and bloody ground" or "meadow land"

Ohio—"good river"

Shenandoah—"daughter of the stars," "big meadow," or "river through the spruces"

Tennessee—from Tanasi, the name of a Cherokee village

In 1838, President Andrew Jackson sent the U.S. Army to the southern Appalachians to evict the Cherokee from their land. From December 1838 to March 1839, 14,000 Cherokee were forced to hike from their homelands to the Oklahoma Territory. As many as 4,000 Cherokee died along the way—mostly children and the elderly. The Cherokee called the march *Nunna-da-ul-tsun-yi,* "the trail where they cried." The Trail of Tears marked the end of Cherokee resistance to white settlement and control of the Appalachians.

Not all of the Cherokee left their Appalachian homeland. About 1,000 hid in the mountains. In 1878, this group, known as the Eastern Band, was granted some land in the Great Smoky Mountains in western North Carolina. The descendants of these Cherokee continue to live in this area.

SEQUOYA

In 1821, a Cherokee leader named Sequoya created a Cherokee language alphabet. The alphabet, made up of eighty-six different characters, allowed the Cherokee to begin reading and writing. Four years later, the tribe began publishing the *Cherokee Phoenix*, the first Native American newspaper.

The Civil War

In December 1860, South Carolina became the first state to secede from the United States. The rest of the Southeastern states quickly followed, forming the Confederate States of America. The mountains of North Carolina, Tennessee, and Virginia, however, remained strongholds of Union support. As many as 80,000 men from these areas fought for the Union during the Civil War (1861–1865).

When Virginia seceded in April 1861, just days after the start of the war, Virginians living in the western part of the state were furious. Those living in the mountains of Virginia had a very different, more difficult lifestyle than did the plantation owners to the east. Many of the western Virginians did not support slavery and did not want to secede from the Union.

In June 1861, Virginians in the western counties formed the Restored Government of Virginia. In October, the western counties voted to form a new state. On June 20, 1863, this new state entered the Union as West Virginia.

For Confederate deserters, the Appalachians of the Southeast served as a hideout. These *bushwhackers*, as they were known, often received the help of the mountain people. The mountaineers gave them food and clothing in return for protection against Confederate tax collectors. Some of the deserters joined together, forming gangs and murdering anyone sent to bring them back.

During the war, many Appalachian areas suffered greatly. The Shenandoah Valley, called the granary of the Confederacy, was destroyed by Union troops under General Philip H. Sheridan in 1864. That same year, Atlanta, Georgia, a city located in the Piedmont Plateau region of the Appalachians, was captured and torched by Union general William T. Sherman.

opposite:
The Cherokee leader, Sequoya, is shown in a painting by Charles Bird King.

THE BATTLE OF CHATTANOOGA

In November 1863, one of the bloodiest battles of the Civil War took place near Lookout Mountain, a peak in the Cumberland Mountains near Chattanooga, Tennessee. During the Battle of Chattanooga, Union troops commanded by General Ulysses S. Grant attacked Confederate soldiers led by General Braxton Bragg. More than 12,000 men were killed during the three-day battle.

Appalachian Economy

Until the 1800s, most people who settled in or around the Appalachians made their livings by subsistence farming. In the 1870s, outside interests began to see that the mountains could be used for profit. The first major industry in the Appalachians was the lumber industry. Tree cutters systematically harvested the mountain forestlands, wiping out old-growth forests and leaving the bare mountainsides exposed to erosion. *Old-growth forests* are forests that have been growing for a very long time. These forests have a diverse and well-developed ecosystem, with unique types of trees, plants, and wildlife. Destroying old-growth forests also destroys these ecosystems.

Later, as railroads into the mountains made transporting goods easier and less costly, other Appalachian businesses sprang up. These businesses included salt mining, as well as glass-, textile-, and furniture-making. Today, these and many other businesses, including iron, aluminum, and steel plants and factories that make chemicals and industrial machines, contribute to the Appalachian economy.

Coal Becomes King

Coal was first discovered in the Appalachians in the early 1700s, but there was then no real need for the mineral. After the Civil War, however, coal became much more important to the U.S. economy. This much-needed commodity powered steam engines and fueled America's Industrial Revolution.

People from outside the mountains quickly realized the potential of this valuable mineral. They came into the area and took advantage of local landowners, buying up land rights for next to nothing. Some locals were paid just pennies an acre (0.4 hectares); others were given a mule or a horse in exchange for their land. By 1900, absentee landowners controlled 90 percent of three counties in West Virginia. These people had little interest in the Appalachian economy, and little of the wealth that they took from the land was reinvested in the Appalachians.

No longer able to farm their own land, many of the people living in the mountains turned to the coal mines to make a living. They joined thousands of other miners, including immigrants from Eastern Europe. Coal camps, located near the mines, were quickly erected and just as quickly taken down when the coal was gone.

Living conditions in the coal camps were poor. The miners lived in small, squalid houses owned by the coal company and bought their goods from the company store. Prices at these stores were often highly inflated by the company. In lean times, some miners had to

THE TENNESSEE VALLEY AUTHORITY

In 1933, the federal government created an agency called the Tennessee Valley Authority (TVA). The TVA built dams and levees (banks to control flooding) along the Tennessee River and in nearby areas. The dams controlled flooding and also powered nearby electricity plants. By bringing electricity to this part of the country, which never had it before, the TVA improved living conditions in the southern Appalachians.

THE DANGERS OF MINING

In the early 1900s, mining was a dangerous occupation. Underground explosions and other accidents were common. During the twentieth century, more than 127,000 U.S. coal miners died as a result of mining accidents. The worst year for miners was 1907, when 3,242 miners were killed on the job. That year, the worst U.S. mining disaster took 362 lives in West Virginia. Although mining today is much safer, miners still have the highest rate of death among those who work in major industries. In addition, black lung disease has disabled and killed thousands of others.

borrow from the company in order to get by and then work to pay off their debts. If a miner died owing the company money, his sons might be forced to work off the debt. Other miners were paid in what was called *scrip*: metal or paper tokens that could be used only at the mining camp.

The coal miners and their families suffered through cycles of boom and bust in the coal industry. When coal was not needed, the local economy fell apart. During bad times, poverty was severe. From 1940 to 1970, millions left the Appalachian area to find better jobs and lives elsewhere.

Appalachian coal helped power the nation's Industrial Revolution and fueled the rapidly growing economy. Today, Appalachian coal mining is still an important industry. About 14 percent of all U.S. coal is mined in West Virginia and Kentucky. Mining is also important in Alabama and Virginia. In recent years, thanks to labor unions and federal regulations, living and working conditions for Appalachian coal miners have improved.

opposite:
Many teenage boys worked in coal mines during the early 1900s. These two boys are shown in a West Virginia mine in 1908.

THE APPALACHIAN REGIONAL COMMISSION

In 1965, Congress created the Appalachian Regional Commission (ARC) to help people living in the southern Appalachians. Over the years, the ARC has spent billions of dollars to improve highways into Appalachian regions stricken by poverty. Better roadways into the area attract tourism and businesses. The ARC has also built and improved health care and educational facilities in the vicinity. Today, the agency continues to help people in the Appalachians.

Today

In recent years, more national attention has been focused on the Appalachian region. Groups such as the Appalachian Regional Commission (ARC) are looking for ways to ease the poverty in which some Appalachian residents still live. In recent years, educational and economic opportunities have enhanced the quality of life for people in the Appalachians.

The unique culture of Appalachian residents has also attracted widespread interest. Efforts have been made to preserve the mountain traditions of square dancing, fiddling, oral history, and quilting. The American Folklife Center at the Library of Congress is just one of many groups that work to preserve Appalachian culture.

Those who enjoy hiking and nature watching love the Appalachians. The Great Smoky Mountains National Park, for example, has the most visitors of all national parks—more than 9 million people each year. The Appalachian Trail, the nation's longest marked footpath, extends more than 2,000 miles (3,200 kilometers) throughout the Appalachians. The trail begins at Springer Mountain in Georgia and continues to Mount Katahdin in Maine.

ORELENA HAWKS PUCKETT

Orelena Hawks Puckett was born in 1837. Married at the age of sixteen, Puckett and her husband lived on Groundhog Mountain in the Blue Ridge Mountains in Virginia. She gave birth to twenty-four children, all of whom died in infancy. A midwife throughout her life, Puckett delivered more than 1,000 Appalachian babies into the world. She died in 1939 at the age of 102.

Atlantic Ocean

2

The Atlantic Ocean is an important geographical feature of the Southeast. The Atlantic played a key role in the settlement, growth, and economy of the region.

Beginning in the 1500s, the Atlantic coast was the site of the earliest settlements in the United States. Many of these early settlements developed into thriving port cities—centers of trade between the United States and other parts of the world. Some important port cities of the Southeast include Norfolk, Virginia; Charleston, South Carolina; Savannah, Georgia; and Miami, Florida.

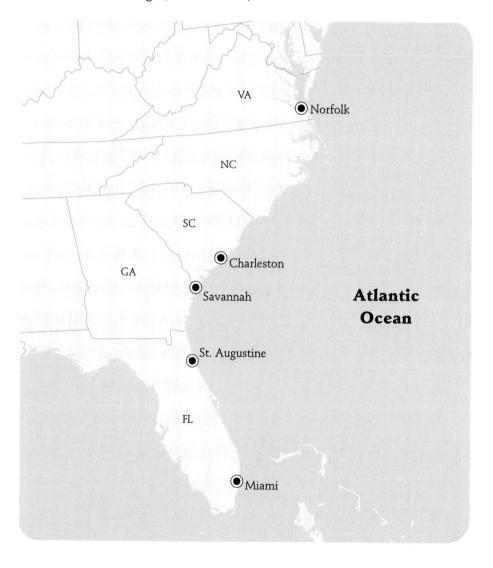

ONE OCEAN, MANY SEAS

The Atlantic Ocean is a vast body of water that contains several other large seas within its boundaries, as shown in this table.

Sea	Size
Arctic Ocean	5,440 square miles (14,144 square kilometers)
Baltic Sea	163 square miles (424 square kilometers)
Black Sea	178 square miles (463 square kilometers)
Caribbean Sea	1,063 square miles (2,764 square kilometers)
Gulf of Mexico	596 square miles (1,550 square kilometers)
Mediterranean Sea	967 square miles (2,514 square kilometers)
North Sea	222 square miles (577 square kilometers)
Norwegian Sea	597 square miles (1,552 square kilometers)

The Atlantic Ocean, nearly 32 million square miles (83.2 million square kilometers) in size, is the second-largest ocean in the world. Only the Pacific Ocean is larger. In the Southeast, the Atlantic coastline stretches for about 1,280 miles (2,048 kilometers) from northern Virginia to the Florida Keys. The tidal shoreline of the Southeast is more than 15,200 miles (24,320 kilometers). This is a measurement of the shorelines of the Atlantic coast's many islands, bays, inlets, and estuaries. (*Estuaries* are places where saltwater from the ocean mixes with freshwater from streams and rivers.)

The Southeast coastline is known for its shallow shoals, sandbars, and many islands. Islands in the Atlantic include the Outer Banks, off North Carolina; the Sea Islands, off Georgia; and the Florida Keys, off the southern tip of Florida. The Southeast's sandy coastline is an area of constant change. Over the years, wind, waves, and currents have shaped the coast. Erosion continues to change the coast today. Bars of sand and mud, beaches, and barrier islands are constantly being created and destroyed.

The climate along the Southeast Atlantic coast varies. States in the north, such as Virginia, enjoy a temperate climate, with mild winters and hot and humid summers. Farther south along the coast, temperatures become even milder. Most of Florida, for example, has a subtropical climate, with very mild winters and very hot and humid summers. From late summer through the fall, hurricanes that form in tropical Atlantic waters can pose a serious threat to the Southeast Atlantic coastline.

Settlement

The Southeast Atlantic coast was first settled about 10,000 years ago by the ancestors of later Native American tribes. At the time of the earliest European settlement, many Native American tribes, including the Tuscarora, Croatoan, Roanoke, and Yamasee, lived in the coastal region. Another important group was the Powhatan Confederacy in the Virginia area. The Powhatan Confederacy was a group of thirty tribes that were led by a chief called Powhatan. According to legend, Powhatan's daughter, Pocahontas, saved English adventurer John Smith from execution. Pocahontas later married John Rolfe, a Jamestown colonist.

The Spanish Were First

In 1565, Spanish explorers founded the first permanent European settlement in the United States. Saint Augustine (San Augustín) was located on the northeast coast of Florida. Although the Spanish attempted to start other settlements along the coast, they were unsuccessful. By 1666, Saint Augustine was the only Spanish settlement on the Atlantic coast. In 1763, the Spanish gave up their claim to Florida to the British.

EARLY SOUTHEAST ATLANTIC EXPLORATION

During the sixteenth century, adventurers from across Europe were exploring the Southeast Atlantic coast.

Explorer	Country	Year	Area Explored
Juan Ponce de León	Spain	1513	Florida
Francisco Gordillo	Spain	1521	South Carolina
Giovanni da Verrazano	France	1524	Atlantic coast from North Carolina to Maine
Lucas Vazques de Ayllón	Spain	1526	Florida, North Carolina
Jean Ribault	France	1562	Florida, South Carolina
Simon Ferdinand	England	1584	Carolinas, Virginia

The English Settle In

The English may not have been the first European settlers on the Southeast Atlantic coast, but they proved to last the longest, and they had the most impact. The first attempt to start an English settlement occurred in 1586, when a group landed on Roanoke Island off the coast of North Carolina. In 1587, the group's leader, John White, sailed back to England for supplies. When he returned to the island three years later, all the houses had been destroyed and the settlers had vanished. No trace of the settlers was ever found, and today Roanoke is called the Lost Colony.

The first permanent English settlement in the New World was established in 1607. In May of that year, three ships crossed the Atlantic and sailed 60 miles (96 kilometers) up the James River in Virginia. They

VIRGINIA DARE

The first European child born in colonial America was Virginia Dare. Born on Roanoke Island in August 1587, Virginia was the granddaughter of John White, the leader of the Roanoke expedition. Virginia and her parents disappeared with the rest of Roanoke's settlers sometime between 1587 and 1590.

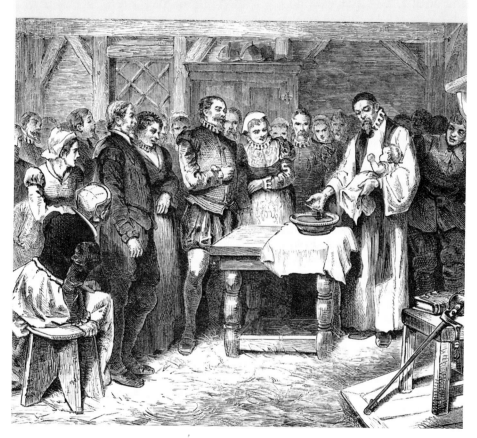

This painting depicts the baptism of Virginia Dare, the first European child born in North America.

founded James Towne, later known as Jamestown. Life for the pioneers was difficult. However, the settlers soon discovered that Virginia's soil was well suited for growing tobacco. Tobacco would soon become the cornerstone of the colony's economy.

English settlement of other coastal areas followed. In 1670, the port city of Charles Towne, later Charleston, became the first settlement in South Carolina. In 1706, one of North Carolina's first towns, Bath, was founded along the Atlantic coast.

The coastal colony of Georgia was established in 1733, when King George II granted James Oglethorpe and several other Englishmen a charter to settle in the New World. The king believed that the new colony would serve as a buffer between the other English colonies to the north and the Spanish settlements to the south. Georgia was to be a place where the poor of England could go to start a new life. Savannah, a city near the Atlantic coast, was Georgia's first European settlement.

JOHN ROLFE AND TOBACCO

Jamestown resident John Rolfe is credited with starting the tobacco industry in Virginia. In 1612, Rolfe planted tobacco seeds that he had imported from the Caribbean. After the tobacco was grown, he cured and barreled the leaves and then shipped them off to England. Over the years, the demand for Virginia tobacco increased dramatically, fueling a thriving economy in the new colony. Rolfe later married Pocahontas, daughter of Chief Powhatan. The marriage ensured peace between the Jamestown colonists and the Powhatan Confederacy for several years.

Commerce on the Southeast Coast

From the earliest colonial days, the English colonies along the Southeast Atlantic coast depended upon farming and shipping to drive their economy. In Virginia, tobacco was the chief crop. The port city of Norfolk was founded in 1682 as a place to store and ship tobacco.

In North Carolina, the chief crops were tobacco and rice. The key crops of South Carolina and Georgia were rice and indigo. Indigo is a plant that is used to make blue dye. Charleston soon became a center of trade in the colonies, shipping out tobacco, rice, indigo, wheat, and cotton. By 1773, Charleston was the largest port south of Philadelphia. Savannah, Georgia, was also an important Southeastern port.

Agriculture and shipping led to the growth of many other businesses along the Southeast coast. Shipbuilding and repair was one industry directly related to the thriving coastal shipping trade. Merchants and artisans also set up businesses in port cities, hoping to cash in on the colonies' newfound wealth.

Not everyone in the colonies benefited from the great riches provided by tobacco, rice, and other crops. The wealthy coastal planters stood in stark contrast to the poor tenant farmers and frontiersmen who lived further inland. These differences in wealth would eventually cause problems between the settlers on the coast and those to the west.

Farming continues to be important along the Southeast Atlantic coast. Tobacco, soybeans, corn, wheat, cotton, peanuts, and peaches are all major crops grown in the area today. Fruits of the sea also support the Southeast economy. Oysters, clams, crabs, shrimps, and saltwater fish are taken from Southeast Atlantic waters and sold around the world.

Plantations and Slavery

• *Fast Fact* •

The first African slaves in the American colonies arrived in Jamestown, Virginia, in 1619. The twenty African men had been taken by the Dutch from a Spanish ship. The men worked in the colonies for several years and then were given their freedom.

As planters along the coast made money selling their crops, they branched out and bought even more land to farm. As their farms grew bigger, they needed more people to work on them. The planters felt that the perfect solution to their labor problems was African slaves. In 1661, Virginia wrote a law that allowed slavery in the colony. A few years later, the Royal African Company began shipping slaves directly from Africa to the Southeast colonies. Norfolk, Virginia, became a major slave port.

CATO'S CONSPIRACY

The first serious slave revolt in the colonies took place near Charleston, South Carolina, in 1739. That September, a slave named Cato led a group of about eighty slaves to attack a store to get weapons. They killed two people in the process. Then the group headed toward St. Augustine, Florida. They were stopped by armed colonists. During the revolt, as many as thirty colonists and forty slaves were killed.

By 1708, the black population in South Carolina outnumbered the white population. Most of the black slaves in the colony worked the rice plantations along the coast. As populations of slaves increased in the Southeast colonies, white colonists began to worry about slave revolts and other conflicts. They began passing laws that more severely limited the way slaves had to behave. For example, slaves were forbidden to bear arms and to learn to read or write.

The plantation economy created an upper class of colonists in the Southeast. Not only were the eastern

THE MIDDLE PASSAGE

Between the seventeenth and nineteenth centuries, an estimated 8 million to 15 million Africans were enslaved and sent to colonial America. The voyage from Africa to the colonies was known as the Middle Passage. Hundreds of slaves were crammed into the holds of slave ships and chained together to prevent escape. The slaves were fed just enough to keep them alive, and diseases such as smallpox and dysentery were common. To prevent the spread of disease in these close quarters, sick slaves were often thrown overboard. As many as one out of every five African slaves died before reaching America.

plantation owners very rich, but they also became very powerful. Soon, plantation masters were running the colonial governments, writing the laws that affected their colonies. This led to resentment and ill will between the plantation masters along the coast and other people who lived in other parts of the colony.

African-American Culture Develops

For slaves, life on the plantations was hard. Most slaves—men, women, and children—spent their lives working in the fields or performing menial tasks around the plantation. A typical workday began at sunup and continued until sundown—sometimes even longer. Slaves planted, hoed, weeded, tended, and picked the fields. After working all day in the fields, slaves went home to small, drafty slave cabins. Some of these dark, dirty quarters were only sixteen square feet (1.4 square meters). Often, one or two families shared a cabin.

While some plantation owners treated their slaves well, many did not. Many slaves were whipped, beaten, or worse. Each day, slaves faced the fear that they would be sold away from the plantation and their families, or that their loved ones would be sold. They also lived with the knowledge that there was no hope of freedom for themselves or their families.

Despite the harsh conditions, slaves throughout the South found ways to maintain their dignity and self-respect. Over the years, slaves developed a distinct culture all their own, neither African nor American, but a mixture of the two. They used music, dance, folk stories, and other means to create an African-American culture. Some slaves even developed their own dialect—a combination of English and various African and European languages.

THE GULLAH CULTURE

The Gullah are a group of African Americans who live on the Sea Islands off South Carolina, Georgia, and northern Florida. Because of the islands' isolated location, slaves who worked on plantations there were able to retain their distinctive culture. Even today, some islanders continue to speak Gullah, a dialect that combines English with several West African languages. As roads and bridges make access to the islands easier for outsiders, the Gullah culture has weakened somewhat.

The Antislavery Movement

As early as 1688, Quakers (KWAY-kerz) in Pennsylvania began speaking out against slavery in America. The Quakers, also called the Society of Friends, were a religious group whose members began migrating to the New World in the 1660s to escape persecution in England. In 1808, the United States banned the importation of slaves from Africa, but the ban had little effect on the Southeast. By this time, the slave industry was self-sustaining. This meant that as the population of U.S.-born slaves increased, the need for slaves from Africa decreased.

In the 1830s, *abolitionists* (ab-uh-LIH-shun-ests), people against slavery, began calling for an end to slavery throughout the United States. Famous abolitionists included Frederick Douglass, a runaway slave; sisters Sarah and Angelina Grimké, who were daughters of a South Carolina slave owner and converts to the Quaker religion; and Harriet Beecher Stowe, author of *Uncle Tom's Cabin*. Hundreds of other Americans spoke out against slavery in the Southeast.

Despite the appeals and attacks of those who were against slavery, plantation owners were determined to keep their way of life. By 1860, there were more than 46,000 plantations throughout the

South. The coastal economy depended upon slaves working in the rice, indigo, tobacco, and cotton fields. The rich, powerful plantation owners were the first to speak of *secession*, the act of breaking away from the Union (the United States). Secession advocates, with their fiery demands for independence, became known as fire-eaters. After Abraham Lincoln's election as president in 1860, South Carolina became the first state to secede from the Union. More Southeast states quickly followed, and in February, the rebel states formed the Confederate States of America. By late May, eleven Southeastern states had left the Union. The stage was set for the most vicious, bloody war in U.S. history.

The bombardment of Fort Sumter in South Carolina, on April 12 and 13, 1861, was the first engagement of the Civil War. The Union Army surrendered the fort after thirty-four hours of fighting.

The Civil War

On April 12, 1861, the first shots of the Civil War (1861–1865) were fired in Charleston, South Carolina. The Confederates demanded the surrender of Fort Sumter, a federal fort in Charleston Harbor. When the commanding officer refused, the rebels opened fire. They shelled the fort for thirty-four hours until the Union commander finally surrendered. No one was killed during the attack.

On the sea, the Confederates lacked the kind of naval power that the Union had. At the beginning of the war, the Union blockaded the entire Southeast coast. Some small southern ships, called *blockade runners*, sometimes managed to get through the blockade. However, the entire region suffered from a lack of food, medicine, and other supplies during the war. The Union also used its naval power to bombard Southeastern coastal cities.

THE BATTLE OF THE IRONCLADS

On March 9, 1862, a battle took place on the Atlantic Ocean that would change naval warfare forever. That morning, the first two ironclad warships, the Confederate *Virginia* and the Union *Monitor*, battled it out off the coast of Virginia. The *Virginia* had actually been a Union ship, the *Merrimack*, which the Confederates had captured earlier. After being covered with iron and renamed, the *Virginia* was sent out to destroy the Union's wooden warships and end the U.S. naval blockade.

During the battle, cannonballs bounced right off the sides of both ships. The battle went on for hours before both sides retreated. Despite the standoff, the debut of ironclad warships was a success. After the battle, wooden warships became obsolete.

In November 1864, Union general William T. Sherman captured and burned the city of Atlanta, Georgia. Then he began his "march to the sea."

Sherman was determined to make the people of the South so horrified by the war that they would never attempt rebellion again. During the 275-mile (440-kilometer) march, Sherman's troops looted, burned, and destroyed everything in their path. When they reached Savannah and the sea, city officials were prepared to surrender immediately rather than risk Atlanta's fate.

In January 1865, Union forces took control of the last Atlantic port left to the Confederates—Wilmington, North Carolina. The Civil War ended on April 9, 1865, when the South surrendered. Southeastern plantation owners had to adjust to a new way of life, after all.

During the war, the federal government had abolished slavery. The Southeast's economy was in ruins. Many plantations had been destroyed, their livestock and crops wiped out. Times were tough for everyone, white and black alike. After the war, large numbers of blacks and former Confederates migrated out of the Southeast. Many former slaves went to the North and to the West. Confederates moved to Mexico, South America, and other places. It would take many years before the Southeast began to recover.

The South and Segregation

After the Civil War ended, black people throughout the United States were free. But in many Southeast states, they were still not treated equally. After the war, some Southeastern states passed "black codes," laws that discriminated against blacks. In the late 1800s and early 1900s, these laws came to be known as "Jim Crow laws."

Jim Crow laws *segregated*, or unfairly separated, whites from blacks in public places. Blacks had to attend separate schools, eat at separate restaurants, and use separate water fountains and public bathrooms. They were not allowed to eat at white lunch counters and were made to sit behind a "color line" at the backs of public buses.

Southern states wanted to keep blacks from electing leaders who would change these unfair laws. Some states used poll taxes to discourage freed blacks from voting. A *poll tax* was a fee that had to be paid before a person was allowed to vote. Other states made voters take a reading test before they could vote. Because most freed blacks were poor and didn't know how to read or write, they could not vote in these states.

Blacks who spoke out against injustices or broke Jim Crow laws were often subject to violent beatings. Some were even killed. Between 1890 and 1960, more than 5,000 blacks were *lynched*, or murdered, by mobs of whites.

During the twentieth century, things slowly changed for black people in the United States. In the 1940s, a series of important court decisions ruled that Jim Crow laws were unconstitutional. Then the 1950s saw the beginnings of the civil rights movement. During the civil rights movement, important national leaders emerged to ask all people to speak up for racial equality.

Civil rights leaders organized protests, rallies, demonstrations, and marches. They attracted national attention to the situation of black people in the United States. National civil rights leaders included Martin Luther King Jr., Malcolm X, Ralph Abernathy, Jesse Jackson, Rosa Parks, and Medgar Evers.

Coastal Perils

From the earliest days of exploration, the Southeast Atlantic coastline has been known as a dangerous place for ships. Shallows, sandbars, and barrier islands make the area treacherous, especially off the Outer Banks of North Carolina. Hundreds of shipwrecks lie beneath the waters of the Southeast Atlantic, earning the area its sinister name, Graveyard of the Atlantic.

During the late 1600s and early 1700s, sailors along the Southeast coast also had to contend with pirates. The coves, inlets, and hidden bays along the coastline gave pirates plenty of hiding places. Some of the most infamous pirates of the period were Anne Bonny, Charles Vane, and Stede Bonnet, also known as the Gentleman Pirate. The most notorious pirate of all, however, was Edward Teach, better known as Blackbeard. Between 1716 and 1718, Blackbeard terrorized ships off Virginia and the Carolinas.

HURRICANE STRIKE ZONE

Beginning in late summer, people along the Southeastern coast listen carefully to weather reports. That's because *hurricanes*—tropical storms that brew in the Southeast Atlantic—can cause serious damage in the area. This table shows some of the Southeast's costliest hurricanes.

Hurricane	Date	Location	Damage	Deaths
Great Miami	September 1926	Florida	$112 million	243
Labor Day	September 1935	Florida Keys	$11 million	408
Hazel	October 1954	Carolinas	$281 million	95
Connie	August 1955	North Carolina	$5.2 million	25
Hugo	September 1989	South Carolina	$7 billion	82
Andrew	August 1992	Florida	$26.5 billion	26
Fran	September 1996	North Carolina	$3.2 billion	34

Lifesaving along the Atlantic

Some of the first efforts to make the Atlantic coast safer for ships included the building of lighthouses in the most dangerous areas. Some of the earliest lighthouses along the Southeast Atlantic included Cape Henry

Lighthouse (1791) and Assateague Lighthouse (1833) in Virginia, Cape Hatteras Lighthouse (1803) in North Carolina, Morris Island Lighthouse (1876) in South Carolina, and St. Simon's Lighthouse (1811) in Georgia.

• Fast Fact •

In the 1880s, the city of Virginia Beach, Virginia, sprang up around four regional lifesaving stations.

The first lighthouse built along the Southeast coast was Tybee Island Lighthouse in Georgia. Erected in 1736, the lighthouse was made of brick and wood. The lighthouse was destroyed by a fierce storm in 1741. A second Tybee Island Lighthouse was finished seven years later.

In the 1700s, "wreckmasters" patrolled sections of the coast. These people, appointed by the coastal states, were required to try to salvage goods and rescue survivors from ships wrecked in their areas. The wreckmasters had to put together a crew of volunteers to help at each wreck.

In 1871, the U.S. Life-Saving Service (USLSS) was born. The group built new lifesaving stations up and down the Atlantic coast. They built stations on the Great Lakes, the Mississippi River, and the Pacific coast, as well. The USLSS cut down on the high number of deaths resulting from shipwrecks up and down the coast. From 1871 to 1914, the USLSS saved more than 178,000 people who were shipwrecked.

In 1915, the USLSS joined with the U.S. Revenue Cutter Service to form a single body: the U.S. Coast Guard. Today, the Coast Guard handles

MIAMI: A PLACE OF REFUGE

At the beginning of the twentieth century, Miami was a haven for vacationers from the North who wanted to escape cold winter weather. Beginning in the 1960s, however, Miami offered refuge of a different sort: People fleeing communist Cuba began settling there. In the summer of 1980 alone, thousands of Cubans came to the city. Today, about 60 percent of Miami's population is Cuban. Spanish, the language of Cuba, is widely spoken in the city.

The Cape Hatteras Lighthouse on the Outer Banks of North Carolina is one of the most recognized symbols of the Southeast coast. the maintenance of lighthouses, light ships, and navigational aids such as buoys. It also continues to save the lives of people who find themselves in danger on the seas. An important service of the Coast Guard is boater safety courses, used to educate recreational boaters about safe boating.

THE FIRST NATIONAL SEASHORE

Cape Hatteras National Seashore, established in 1953, was the nation's first national seashore. The seashore covers more than 70 miles (112 kilometers) of shoreline and protects three Outer Banks islands. Visitors to Cape Hatteras National Seashore can enjoy more than 30,000 acres (12,000 hectares) of sandy beaches, dunes, and salt marshes. The seashore is also home to the nation's tallest lighthouse, Cape Hatteras Lighthouse. This tower is 198 feet (59.4 meters) high. When it was first built in 1870, the lighthouse was 1,500 feet (450 meters) from the ocean. Over the years, the wind and tides whittled the distance down to just 100 feet (30 meters). In 1999, the lighthouse was moved. It now sits 1,600 feet (480 meters) from the sea.

Henry Flagler and Tourism

Although Florida was the first U.S. state to be settled by Europeans, it remained sparsely populated until the late 1800s. In 1883, developer Henry M. Flagler spent the winter on the east coast of Florida. Flagler decided that he would turn Florida's Atlantic coast into a winter haven for people from up north. He built hotels, resorts, and railroads from Jacksonville all the way to the Florida Keys. He used his railroad, the Florida East Coast Railway, to link towns up and down the state's Atlantic coast. Thanks to Flagler, such places as Palm Beach and Miami became world-famous tourist towns.

The first coastal Florida town that Flagler turned his attention to was St. Augustine. This was the site of the first permanent European settlement in the United States. In 1888, the millionaire opened up the Ponce de Leon Hotel there. Flagler's next project was to develop a town solely for rest and relaxation. He chose a barrier island off Florida's southeastern coast: Palm Beach.

To attract the rich and famous to Palm Beach, Flagler built several huge luxury hotels. The Breakers and the Royal Poinciana were two of the earliest—and the grandest—of Flagler's hotels along the Atlantic coast. Although the Breakers was destroyed by a fire in 1903, Flagler quickly had the hotel rebuilt, bigger and better than before.

Palm Beach soon became the winter vacation hot spot for millionaires from around the nation. Many, including Flagler himself, built enormous homes there. Flagler's home, called Whitehall, was located on 6 acres (2.4 hectares) of seaside property and had seventy-three rooms. Today, Whitehall is a museum for Palm Beach visitors.

In 1896, Miami landowner Julia Tuttle convinced Flagler to extend the Florida East Coast Railway from Palm Beach to Miami. Tuttle pointed out that while

Palm Beach had freezing temperatures at the time, Miami was still nice and warm. After a visit to the sunny southern region, Flagler agreed, and the train soon chugged into Miami.

Flagler next turned his eyes to the Florida Keys. He wanted to build a huge railroad across the water to connect Miami to the sea islands. Flagler lived just long enough to ride once on his Key West Railway in 1912. The following year, he died in West Palm Beach at the age of eighty-three. Today, a town and a county in Florida are both named for the man who started the state's vacation boom.

A CARGO OF COCONUTS

In 1878, the Spanish ship *Providencia* was wrecked off the Atlantic coast of Florida. The ship, bound for Spain from the West Indies, was carrying a cargo of rum and thousands of coconuts. Many of the seeds took root and grew wild. Local villagers planted many others, hoping to harvest and sell the coconuts. Soon the area was covered with coconut palm trees and earned the name Palm Beach.

Miami Takes Off

Like other Atlantic coast cities in Florida, Miami can thank Henry Flagler for its start. Miami, located on the site of an old U.S. fort built in 1836, officially became a town on July 28, 1896. That same year, Flagler extended his railway line to the new city and opened the Royal Palm Hotel there. He also began dredging Miami's harbor, making it deeper and better for large boats.

The city quickly grew into a popular resort area. In the early 1900s, developers improved on what Flagler had started. Miami experienced a building boom in the 1920s that lasted until the Great

Depression hit the nation at the end of that decade. The Great Depression was the most serious economic crisis in the nation's history.

After World War II (1939–1945), Miami bounced back. Today, the city is one of the largest in Florida. It is a booming port town that relies heavily on tourism. Several cruise lines dock in Miami Harbor. The city also has a large population of Cuban-American residents, which gives Miami a unique cultural heritage.

WHAT'S IN A NAME?

Miami was almost called Flagler! In 1896, residents asked Henry Flagler if they could name their town for him. Flagler declined. He suggested that they call the town Miami, the name that native tribes had given the area. *Miami* means "sweet water."

Today's Coast

Tourism is important to other parts of the Southeast Atlantic coast, too. Each year, millions of vacationers visit Virginia Beach in Virginia; Myrtle Beach and Hilton Head in South Carolina; the Outer Banks in North Carolina; and the Sea Islands off the coast of Florida.

Visitors are also attracted by the Southeast's rich coastal history. Scuba divers, for example, can check out the many wrecks off the coast of North Carolina. People interested in aviation visit Kill Devil Hill, near the village of Kitty Hawk on the Outer Banks, where, in 1903, brothers Wilbur and Orville Wright made the very first airplane flight in history. Those more interested in the future of flight can watch a space shuttle take off from Cape Canaveral on Merritt Island in Florida.

As more and more people come to love the Southeastern Atlantic coast, a balance must be found. Overdevelopment and ever increasing numbers of tourists threaten the waters, beaches, and surrounding ecosystems. In recent years, people living along the Southeastern coast have tried to control development more carefully and find ways to protect and preserve the coastline.

Bluegrass Region

3

The Bluegrass Region is an area in north-central Kentucky. It is a fertile, grassy area of gently sloping hills and plains. The Bluegrass Region gets its name from the type of grass that grows there.

The Bluegrass Region covers about one-fifth of the entire state of Kentucky. The area has played an important role in the state's history and economic growth. Many of Kentucky's most important cities are located in the Bluegrass Region, including Frankfort, Lexington-Fayette, and Louisville. Frankfort is Kentucky's capital, while Lexington-Fayette and Louisville are the state's two most populous cities.

Settlement

The first humans to settle in the Bluegrass area arrived more than 12,000 years ago. These ancestors of later Native American groups hunted the wild animals that roamed the forests of the region. Later tribes who claimed the right to hunt there included the Shawnee, Cherokee, Chickasaw, and Iroquois. Some of the tribes blazed paths westward across the Appalachians from the Atlantic coast to take advantage of the fertile hunting grounds.

During early colonial days, the Appalachians were a barrier for European colonists who had settled along the Atlantic coast. As the coastal areas became more and more crowded, however, colonists began looking for new land. Before long, enterprising adventurers began wondering what lay beyond the massive mountains to the west.

One of the first colonists to look for a path through the Appalachians was Dr. Thomas Walker. In 1750, Walker discovered the Cumberland Gap. The gap is a narrow pass that begins where the states of Virginia, Tennessee, and Kentucky meet. In a matter of years, the Cumberland Gap became one of the chief passages to the western frontier.

BLUEGRASS?

How did Kentucky bluegrass get its name? For a short time in the spring, this variety of grass looks blue in color when hit by the morning sun. "Kentucky" bluegrass is actually from Europe. Some historians believe that the grass, first known as June grass, arrived in America in the early 1600s. It may have been mixed in with grain for cattle and other livestock.

Bluegrass is a strong grass that spreads quickly and grows year-round. Today, it is one of the most common types of grass in the United States. Because bluegrass does well in cold temperatures and grows all year, it is especially popular in the northern part of the nation.

Kentucky horse and cattle farmers like their animals to eat bluegrass, because it contains minerals that help them grow strong. The grass also grows back quickly, making it ideal for pastureland.

The first permanent settlement west of the Allegheny (al-uh-GAYN-ee) Mountains was founded in the Bluegrass Region in 1774. That year, James Harrod of Pennsylvania settled in what he named Harrodstown. Today, the town is known as Harrodsburg.

In 1775, Daniel Boone made his way through the Cumberland Gap with a group of thirty men. Boone and his crew created a pathway from the gap up through central Kentucky. The trail soon became known as the Wilderness Road. The Wilderness Road was the first practical trail from the East Coast to the Kentucky frontier.

Boaters enjoy the Kentucky River near Boonesboro, Kentucky. In addition to the town, a state park near Boonesboro is named in honor of the famous explorer.

The Kentucky frontier was not new territory for Boone. In 1769, he had journeyed through the Cumberland Gap and into Kentucky to hunt. Apparently, Boone liked what he saw. On his second trip into the area, he built Fort Boonesborough, located just south of what is now Lexington. Today, the town where Boone built his fort is known as Boonesboro.

After the opening of the Wilderness Road, thousands of people from the crowded Atlantic coast settled in Kentucky. Most early Kentuckians were English, Scottish, and Scotch-Irish from Virginia, Tennessee, and North Carolina. Kentucky became known as one of the gateways to the West.

DANIEL BOONE, TRAILBLAZER

Daniel Boone is perhaps the most famous trailblazer and pioneer in American history. Born in Pennsylvania in 1734, Boone and his family moved to North Carolina when he was a teenager. In 1775, Boone was hired by the Transylvania Land Company to establish a pathway into the area that would come to be known as Kentucky.

Boone eventually moved his entire family with him to Kentucky. They faced many hardships, including attacks by hostile Native Americans. Boone himself was even taken hostage by a group of natives in 1778.

Boone and his wife Rebecca remained in Kentucky for thirteen years before moving first to West Virginia and then to Missouri. Boone died in Missouri at the age of eighty-five. But both he and his wife are buried in Frankfort, in the state that they helped to settle.

Settling Bluegrass Cities

In 1775, an important Kentucky milestone took place: The town of Lexington was founded by Robert Patterson and seven other men. The group named the settlement for Lexington, Massachusetts, the scene of the first real battle of the American Revolution

(1775–1783). Although the site was abandoned the following year, Patterson returned to permanently settle there in 1779.

As more and more people began crossing the Appalachian Mountains into Kentucky, many of them realized that the Bluegrass Region was the perfect place to settle down. The land itself was open, flat, and fertile. In addition, there was a plentiful supply of water in the area, thanks to the many rivers and streams.

When Kentucky was allowed into the Union in 1792, Lexington was named its temporary capital. By the 1820s, it had become one of the largest cities west of the Alleghenies. People throughout the United States called Lexington the "Athens of the West" because of the many cultural and social activities that took place there. (The city of Athens had been the center of art and culture in ancient Greece.)

Later, the city of Frankfort in the Bluegrass Region was chosen as Kentucky's capital. Founded in 1786 by the Virginia Assembly, Frankfort's central location in the new state made it the ideal site for the capital. Frankfort was named for pioneer Stephen Frank, who was killed in the area, fighting Native Americans.

• Fast Fact •

THE BOY SCOUTS OF AMERICA

The first U.S. Boy Scout troop was organized in Frankfort, Kentucky, in 1908.

A third important city in the Bluegrass Region is Louisville. Louisville was founded in 1778 by George Rogers Clark. Clark was the older brother of William Clark, who would go on to fame as half of the Lewis and Clark expedition. (The Lewis and Clark expedition was the first group sent out by the U.S. government to explore the territory west of the Mississippi.) The settlement was named after King Louis XVI of France, who helped the United States during the American Revolution.

The Civil War

In the 1860s, the debate over slavery in the United States began to heat up. Just as the United States was divided over this important issue, so was the Bluegrass Region of Kentucky. Kentucky was a border state, straddling the North and South. While many people in the region believed that slavery was wrong, many others were slaveholders themselves. Families in the region found themselves torn apart by strife and dissent.

When the Civil War (1861–1865) began, Kentucky declared that it was a neutral state. State politicians decided to stay with the Union. Outraged Confederate supporters set up their own, alternate government in Bowling Green, Kentucky. Rebel forces held Bowling Green for little more than a year before being defeated by Union troops. By the time the war was over, more than 80,000 Kentuckians had fought for the Union, while nearly 35,000 had fought for the Confederacy.

FAMOUS FOLKS OF LEXINGTON

Mary Todd Lincoln, wife of President Abraham Lincoln, was a Bluegrass native. Born in Lexington in 1818, she lived there until she was twenty-one years old. Then she moved to Springfield, Illinois, where she met the young lawyer she would soon marry.

Henry Clay, a famous politician and orator, tried to stop the Civil War before it began. His attempts to reconcile the two sides earned him the nickname "The Great Compromiser." Clay, one of Abraham Lincoln's mentors, ran unsuccessfully for president three times. He once said, "I would rather be right than be president."

William Wells Brown, born into slavery in the Bluegrass Region, escaped to the North in 1834. Eight years later, he wrote the *Narrative of William Wells Brown, A Fugitive Slave, Written by Himself.* Brown also wrote several other works of literature. Before the Civil War broke out, Brown helped many other slaves escape from slavery in the South.

Commerce

From the beginning of colonial settlement in the Bluegrass Region, one of the area's chief draws was its rich, fertile farmland. The Bluegrass Region has some of the best land in the United States for growing crops and grazing livestock. Because of the area's plentiful pastures and water sources, farmers and ranchers who settled in the area thrived.

The Bluegrass Region quickly became prosperous. Before the Civil War, hemp was the area's chief crop. Hemp is a plant with very strong, durable fibers. It can be used to make rope, clothing, and other items. Kentucky farmers sold their hemp to merchants in New England. These merchants used the hemp fibers to make ropes for the many ships being built. By 1840, Kentucky produced more hemp than any other state in the nation.

BOURBON COUNTRY

The Bluegrass Region is sometimes called "Bourbon Country." *Bourbon* is a kind of whiskey that is made with corn and rye. The first bourbon may have been made in 1789 by Elijah Craig, a Baptist minister in the Bluegrass Region. One of the first bourbon *distilleries*, or factories, was built near Louisville in 1793. Today, Kentucky bourbon is made in Louisville, Frankfort, Lexington, and several other Bluegrass cities.

Tobacco

The crop that would prove to be the mainstay of the Bluegrass economy was tobacco (tuh-BAK-oh). Although tobacco was grown in Kentucky as early as the 1780s, it was not then an important crop. After the Civil War, however, things changed. In 1864, a new, hardier strain of tobacco, called *burley tobacco*, was developed in Ohio. Kentucky farmers soon found that burley tobacco was perfect for Kentucky's soil and climate.

Burley tobacco quickly became the area's number-one crop. Beginning in 1865, Frankfort and

Lexington became centers for the tobacco trade. Until 1929, Kentucky was the top tobacco-producing state in the nation.

Today, tobacco remains the most important cash crop in Kentucky. The state is second only to North Carolina in tobacco production. Lexington continues to be one of the major cities for the trade in tobacco. Each year, millions of pounds of the plant are sold in the city.

This tobacco cutter in Sulphur Well, Kentucky, harvests his crop in much the same way it has been harvested for hundreds of years.

Jockey Ron Turcotte rides Secretariat during the ninety-ninth Kentucky Derby at Churchill Downs near Louisville, Kentucky. Secretariat went on to win the Triple Crown in 1973.

Horses and Racing

For many people, Kentucky Bluegrass means Thoroughbred horses and horse racing. The area is known throughout the world as the center of Thoroughbred horse breeding. The nutrient-rich grass and temperate climate of the region are perfect for raising racehorses. As a result, hundreds of horse farms are located in the Bluegrass Region. Each year, thousands of horses are bred—and sold—here. One of the world's most famous horse races, the Kentucky Derby, is held each May in Louisville.

The first Thoroughbred horse was brought to Kentucky in 1779. Before long, horse owners in Lexington, Louisville, and other Bluegrass towns were racing through city streets to see whose horse was the fastest. In 1789, Lexington became the site of the first racetrack in the state.

By the turn of the century, Thoroughbreds were being bred and raced throughout the Bluegrass Region. In 1875, Kentucky banker M. Lewis Clark opened Churchill Downs, a racetrack for horses, in Louisville. There, in May, the first Kentucky Derby was run.

Since 1875, the famous Kentucky Derby has been held on the first Saturday each May. The race itself lasts only about two minutes, but people come from around the world to celebrate it. Traditional festivities, starting weeks before the race, include a hat parade, mint juleps (a drink consisting of bourbon or brandy, sugar, and mint leaves over crushed ice), and the singing of Kentucky's state song, "My Old Kentucky Home."

Today, the derby is part of horse racing's "Triple Crown." The Triple Crown is made up of the three most important Thoroughbred races in the country. The other two races are the Preakness Stakes in Maryland and the Belmont Stakes in New York.

Horse racing and breeding continue to be big business in Kentucky. At the Kentucky Horse Park in

Man O' War celebrates his thirtieth birthday on March 29, 1947.

KENTUCKY'S MOST FAMOUS HORSE

Man O' War, one of the most successful racehorses in history, was born near Lexington, Kentucky, on March 29, 1917. From 1919 to 1920, Man O' War dominated horse racing. During his amazing career, Man O' War won twenty out of twenty-one races and earned his owners more than $240,000—a large sum for the time. When Man O' War died in 1947, he lay in state for three days. About 2,000 people came to bid the famous horse farewell.

Lexington, Thoroughbreds from around the world are trained. The park is also home to the Man O' War memorial and the International Museum of the Horse.

Other Bluegrass Industry

In the twentieth century, manufacturing and industry became an important part of the Bluegrass Region's economy. Today, metal goods, auto parts, processed food, electronics, and paper products are all made in the area.

One famous item manufactured in the Bluegrass Region is the Louisville Slugger baseball bat. Made in Louisville since 1884, these bats are still used by baseball players across the country. The official bats of Major League Baseball, Louisville Sluggers are used by about 60 percent of all major league players. Famous players who have batted with Louisville Sluggers include Honus Wagner, Ty Cobb, Babe Ruth, and Sammy Sosa.

Today

Industry and agriculture both still play a major role in the Bluegrass Region economy. The tobacco industry, for example, is still an important part of Kentucky's economy. However, as tobacco has become more controversial and less popular in recent years, the number of tobacco farms in the region has decreased. Those who farm tobacco in Kentucky and elsewhere may soon have to find other ways of making a living.

Today, the Bluegrass Region is the most highly populated and prosperous section of Kentucky. Louisville is the state's largest city, while Lexington-Fayette is the second largest. The continued growth of the region places a strain on the surrounding environment. As more people move into an area, pollution and overcrowding can become problems. A future challenge for those living in the area will be to keep the Bluegrass Region free of pollution.

As early as 1979, the state of Kentucky began setting aside wild areas in the Bluegrass Region. Today, the area is home to nine state nature preserves. These preserves ensure that the wild areas of Kentucky will remain for people to enjoy in the coming years.

Everglades

4

The Everglades is a large freshwater marsh that covers 5 million square miles (13 million square kilometers) in southern Florida. This slow-moving, shallow sheet of water begins just south of Lake Okeechobee and runs southwest to the Gulf of Mexico. Water overflowing from the lake supplies the Everglades with its fresh water. Everglades National Park is located within its boundaries.

The Everglades is one of the least accessible places in the nation. It is covered with thick saw grass that rises 3 to 10 feet (0.9 to 3 meters) above the surface. Cypress, mangrove, palm, oak, and bay trees make up some of the natural vegetation in the area. The Everglades is home to a wide variety of wildlife, including panthers, loggerhead turtles, manatees, and many species of birds.

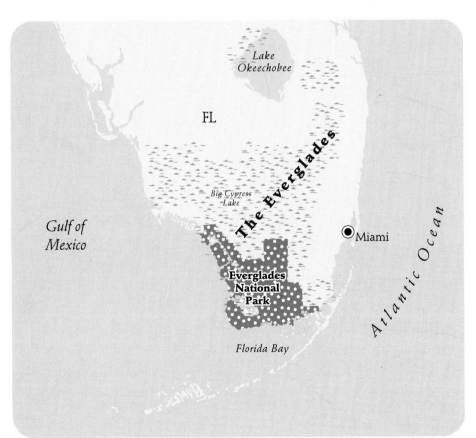

A RIVER OF GRASS

Marjory Stoneman Douglas was a writer who spent most of her life working to save the Everglades. In 1947, she wrote the book *The Everglades: A River of Grass*, describing the vital wetlands. Over the years, Douglas campaigned tirelessly to prevent development and other damage to the Everglades. She died in 1998 at the age of 108.

Airboats make travel over the shallow, grassy waters of the Everglades much easier than using conventional boats, whose propellers can become tangled in the mud and weeds.

Settlement

The Everglades is young, geologically speaking. Scientists believe that these swampy wetlands formed only about 5,000 years ago, long after the last Ice Age had ended. Melting glacier waters filled the shallow limestone basin that the Everglades rests upon today. Peat and other wetland soils built up in the area, creating the marshy region.

Even before the Everglades existed, people were living in the south Florida area. These ancestors of later Native American groups arrived as early as 12,000 years ago. Later, two of the most important tribes in the Everglades area were the Calusa (kuh-LOO-suh) and the Tequesta. These tribes hunted and fished in the area, catching deer and shellfish.

The first European explorers, the Spanish, arrived in the early 1500s. At this time, there were perhaps 20,000 native people living in the area. Over the next 250 years, however, these native tribes virtually disappeared, wiped out by European diseases and slavery.

In the 1700s, groups of Creek natives from Alabama, Georgia, and the Carolinas arrived in Florida, driven from their land by the colonists up north. These different groups of Creeks became known collectively as the Seminoles. *Seminole* comes from the Spanish word *cimmaron*, which means "wild" or "runaway." The Seminoles at first settled in north Florida.

After the American Revolution (1775–1783), the British returned Florida to the Spanish. The Seminoles thought that they were safe from American settlers there, but Americans soon began looking at Florida as the newest place to expand. The Seminoles also earned the wrath of southern plantation owners by sheltering runaway African slaves.

The Seminole Wars

In the 1800s, violence erupted between Seminoles and American settlers. The first Seminole War (1817–1818) began when General Andrew Jackson invaded Spanish-controlled north Florida and defeated the natives. He also took control of Pensacola, a Spanish settlement. Spain eventually ceded Florida to the United States in 1821.

In 1830, Jackson, who had become U.S. president, passed the Indian Removal Act. The act required Native American people to move west to the new Indian Territory in what is now Oklahoma. The second Seminole War (1835–1842) began when some Seminoles resisted the move.

In 1842, about 3,000 Seminoles were sent west, but a handful of others remained behind. As many as 300 Seminoles fled into the Everglades. They were certain that the Americans would not follow them, and they were right. Americans viewed the swampy marsh as a useless wasteland. They left these last Seminoles alone. Today, several hundred descendants of these peoples still live in the Everglades area.

• Fast Fact •

In 1970, the U.S. government awarded the Seminole people more than $12 million for the land that had been so violently taken from them.

WHAT'S A CHICKEE?

A chickee is a platform dwelling that stands on stilts. Chickees were first constructed by Seminoles who took shelter in the swampy Everglades. They quickly realized that there was little solid ground in the area. The Seminoles built their homes out of cypress logs and palm leaves. Visitors to Everglades National Park can spend a night in one of these dwellings.

Commerce

As early as the mid-1800s, people began looking for a way to make the Everglades useful and profitable. In 1909, developers began draining and dredging parts of the northern Everglades to get at the rich soil below.

As the land south of Lake Okeechobee was drained of water, agriculture became an important part of the area economy. In the 1920s, farmers began planting crops of fruits and vegetables. The most lucrative crop was sugarcane. Over the years, however, fertilizer runoff from sugarcane fields has polluted nearby waterways with high levels of phosphorous, nitrates, and other chemicals.

> • Fast Fact •
>
> **Lake Okeechobee is the fourth-largest lake completely within the boundaries of the United States.**

The area's newfound prosperity attracted more and more people. Towns in south Florida popped up quickly. To provide these new towns with water, canals were built that diverted fresh water from Lake Okeechobee. Flood control to protect the towns boomed in the 1940s, when the Army Corps of Engineers expanded drainage works. Over the next few years, 1,000 miles (1,600 kilometers) of canals, 700 miles (1,120 kilometers) of *levees*, and other water control structures prevented floods and diverted

Tourists aboard a tram at the Shark Valley Visitors Center in the Everglades National Park get a firsthand look at a large alligator sunning itself.

fresh water to nearby towns for drinking. The reduction in fresh water into the Everglades has threatened some plant and fish populations. In addition, less fresh water from the lake has allowed saltwater from the sea to seep into the area, threatening the health of the freshwater marsh.

Tourism is another industry that has both helped and harmed the Everglades. In the 1860s, the railroad made transportation into the swampy wilderness much easier. As more people experienced the unique, marshy ecosystem, interest in visiting and preserving the region grew. Soon, roads were cut through the Everglades to further open up access to the area. Today, about 1 million people visit the Everglades each year.

However, the roads themselves have caused some problems. The highways that slice through the Everglades disrupt the delicate swamp ecosystem, creating artificial dikes that slow the flow of fresh water through the area. In addition, wild animals are sometimes hit and killed by speeding cars on the roads.

THE LAKE OKEECHOBEE HURRICANE

In September 1928, a hurricane roared through central Florida. Lake Okeechobee overflowed its banks and more than 1,800 people in the area drowned. One town was completely wiped out by the flooding except for a handful of buildings left standing. The hurricane set in motion a massive effort of flood control in the area. A big *levee,* or bank, was built on the south side of the lake to prevent another such disaster. Unfortunately, the dike had a negative effect on the Everglades. The natural flow of fresh water that kept the Everglades ecosystem healthy was disrupted. The resulting shortage of water in the Everglades has harmed plants and wildlife in the area.

EVERGLADES NATIONAL PARK

In December 1947, President Harry S. Truman dedicated Everglades National Park. With more than 1.5 million acres (600,000 hectares) of swamps, forests, and marshes, the national park is home to pelicans, panthers, alligators, and manatees. The park has been recognized by conservation groups around the world as a site of international importance, worthy of being preserved.

Today

Environmentalists recognize that the Everglades is an area under siege. Development, tourism, and agriculture have all wreaked havoc on the area. Today, the Everglades is only about half its original size. In addition, 1 million acres (400,000 hectares) are affected by mercury contamination.

In recent years, government officials have offered money to sugar growers to leave the area. This has cut down on the number of sugar plantations in the Everglades, reducing agricultural pollution there. In 1999, state officials began the Florida Forever program. The following year, the federal government passed the Everglades Restoration bill. Over the next twenty years, these two programs will utilize billions of dollars to try to save one of our nation's most precious and unique natural resources.

Florida Keys

5

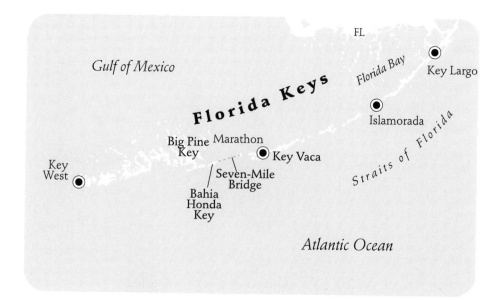

The Florida Keys are a chain of more than 1,700 low-lying coral and limestone islands and reefs between Florida Bay to the north and the Straits of Florida to the south. The word key comes from the Spanish word *cayo,* which means "quay." A quay is a safe place for boats to dock. The keys stretch about 180 miles (288 kilometers) from the island of Virginia Key in Biscayne Bay near Miami southwest to the island of Key West. Key West, in the Gulf of Mexico, is just 90 miles (144 kilometers) north of Cuba. It is the southernmost city in the United States. Other well-known keys include Key Largo, Sugarloaf Key, Bahia Honda Key, Big Pine Key, and Islamorada.

The keys are home to the only living coral reefs in the United States. The Upper Keys themselves are coral in origin. They began forming hundreds of thousands of years ago. These coral islands extend more than 100 miles (160 kilometers), from Soldier Key to Big Pine Key.

• Fast Fact •

The Straits of Florida is a channel of water that connects the Gulf of Mexico to the Atlantic Ocean. The Florida Keys lie to the north of the Straits, while Cuba lies to the south.

The Lower Keys are made of oolite (OH-uh-lite), a type of limestone. They extend about 40 miles (64 kilometers), from Big Pine Key to Key West. The Lower Keys are smaller than the Upper Keys. Coral and algae continue building both the Upper and Lower Keys.

CORAL REEFS

Coral is a living organism, an invertebrate with a hard outer skeleton. Reef-building corals live in shallow seas. They need clear, warm water to thrive. When corals die, they leave behind their skeletons. New corals attach to the dead skeletons, building up the ridge of coral known as a reef. Coral reefs are formed by this ongoing process of dying and growing.

This close-up view shows gamete bundles inside sea coral as they are released into the water off the Florida Keys during the annual spawning.

Settlement

The first people to venture onto the Florida Keys were early Native Americans. These people explored the keys thousands of years before the first Europeans arrived. In the 1500s, the Calusa (kuh-LOO-suh) were one of the most important tribes that lived and fished off the keys. They controlled the southwest region of Florida. By the mid-1700s, however, the Calusa had disappeared from the keys—and the rest of Florida—completely.

The first Europeans to explore the keys were Spanish adventurers. In 1513, Ponce de León sighted the small islands. He dubbed them *Los Martires,* or "the Martyrs," because they seemed to be "like men who were suffering."

The Spanish didn't settle on the keys. However, they did carefully map the islands and surrounding waters. The Spaniards learned the hard lesson that hundreds more would learn over the next centuries: The keys, with their shallow reefs and sand shoals, were a dangerous place for sailors.

The keys' deadly reputation was responsible for attracting the first nonnative settlers on the islands. In the late 1700s and early 1800s, "wreckers" from the Bahamas and New England came to the keys to take advantage of the large number of ships that were wrecked each year off the island shores. Wreckers were people who *salvaged*, or recovered, goods from a shipwreck.

Settlements Spring Up

The first permanent settlement in the keys was Key West. Key West was founded in 1822, the same year that the United States took possession of the keys from Spain. The new town had an excellent deepwater harbor, and for this reason, it quickly became an important U.S. port.

In the 1870s, Americans began settling on the other keys. These people engaged in wrecking, farming, and fishing. Farmers grew coconuts, limes, pineapples, and melons. These "exotic" fruits were sent by ship to such northern ports as Boston and New York.

Hurricane Territory

Because of their location, the keys are sometimes in the paths of violent tropical storms and fierce hurricanes. In past years, these wild storms have killed off coral, destroyed buildings, and altered the look of the islands. Hurricanes have also caused significant loss of life on the keys.

People who live in the keys must be prepared for hurricanes. They listen to weather reports so that they can quickly evacuate the area if a storm is on the way. In a weather emergency, residents can head to hurricane shelters located throughout the islands where they can wait out the storm.

Three residents battle winds of 90 miles (144 kilometers) per hour along Houseboat Row in Key West, Florida. Hurricane George descended on Key West in 1998 and forced many residents to seek shelter.

HISTORIC KEYS HURRICANES

The 1935 Labor Day Hurricane was not the only big storm to threaten the keys. Here are a few other famous ones.

1622 In September, eight Spanish and Portuguese ships sank during a violent hurricane. More than 500 people went down with the ships, along with tons of gold, silver, and other booty. One of the ships, the *Atocha*, was discovered by treasure hunter Mel Fisher in 1985.

1733 In July, nearly the entire fleet of twenty-one Spanish ships was wrecked off the keys. Three of the nineteen ships that sank were the *San Pedro*, the *San Jose*, and the *Infante*. A huge amount of treasure was lost with the ships.

1846 On October 11, a hurricane blew through the town of Key West. Two lighthouses were completely destroyed, and about twenty ships were wrecked. Only eight houses in the town were not damaged or destroyed.

1910 An October hurricane roared across the Straits of Florida from Cuba to Key West. By the time it was over, the town was flooded with 7 feet (2.1 meters) of water.

After a hurricane has hit, the residents of the keys do what generations before them have done: pick up the pieces. They repair damaged roads, bridges, and buildings, and life returns to normal. Despite the dangers of hurricane, many residents say that there is nowhere else that they would rather live.

One of the most disastrous hurricanes to strike the keys was the Labor Day Hurricane of 1935. On September 2, the big storm blew into the keys. Wind speed was estimated at more than 200 miles (320 kilometers) per hour, and waves reached 18 feet (5.4 meters) in height. Homes and other buildings were destroyed—many washed away completely. On Matecumbe Key, not a single building or tree was left standing.

The most tragic episode of the hurricane took place on Islamorada. As people boarded a train sent to evacuate them from the keys, a gigantic wave slammed into the train. The train was washed off the track and onto its side, and hundreds of people were killed. Many of those who were killed were veterans of World War I (1914–1918) who were working on building projects on the keys.

In all, more than 400 people died during the hurricane. The disaster also spelled the end for the Overseas Railroad. Weather experts say that the 1935 Labor Day Hurricane was the strongest hurricane to hit the United States in recorded history. Today, a monument on Islamorada memorializes those who died during the violent storm.

Commerce

Even before they were settled, the Florida Keys were being used by people for their natural resources. In the 1700s, men traveled from the Bahamas to cut down the valuable timber that grew on the islands. These early lumberjacks took mahogany, lignum vitae, and other exotic woods. By 1770, many of the most desirable trees had been completely cleared from the keys.

When people began making their homes on the keys, they turned to the sea to make a living. Fishermen took mackerel and other fish from the waters around the keys. Some early settlers even caught manatees for food. *Manatees*, also called "sea cows," are large mammals that live in the warm, shallow waters off Florida's coasts.

THE DRY TORTUGAS

The Dry Tortugas are ten coral keys in the Gulf of Mexico. Located 70 miles (112 kilometers) west of Key West, the Tortugas are part of Florida. They were first discovered by Ponce de León in 1513. De León named the islands the *Tortugas*, or "turtles," for the turtle meat he and his crew were able to obtain there. The Tortugas are uninhabited and accessible only by sea or air.

Fort Jefferson National Monument and Dry Tortugas National Park are located on Garden Key in the Tortugas. Fort Jefferson was built in 1846 to protect the Straits of Florida. Fort Jefferson served as a Union prison during the Civil War (1861–1865) and then as a federal prison after the war. In 1908, the United States designated the Dry Tortugas as a bird sanctuary.

Shipwrecks and Wreckers

The reefs and sand shoals off the keys can be treacherous for sailors. The waters around the keys are littered with the skeletons of Spanish, English, American, and other ships. One of the first lucrative industries on the keys—wrecking—took advantage of these tragedies.

Some of the earliest wreckers were native peoples hired by the Spanish to salvage goods after the Spanish fleet sank in the 1622 hurricane. From the 1700s to the late 1800s, wrecking was the chief industry in the Florida Keys.

Wreckers operated by waiting for a ship to run aground on the treacherous reefs around the keys. They usually didn't have long to wait: Shipwrecks and ship groundings were common occurrences in the Straits of Florida. Once a ship in trouble had been sighted, wreckers would row out, rescue the crew, and empty the ship's hold. The wreckers made a living by selling the goods that they recovered.

Many of the wreckers were Bahamians—British people who had moved to the islands of the Bahamas—or New Englanders who had moved to the keys in search of riches. Many found their fortunes in the keys: During the 1700s, millions of dollars worth of wrecked goods were salvaged and sold there.

Key West was the center of the wrecking trade. It was here that a federal court, known as the "wrecking court," ruled on disputes between wreckers and ship owners. The wrecking court, following thirteen laws, divided salvaged goods between wreckers and owners. As the wreckers grew rich and prosperous, so did Key West.

In the early 1800s, the construction of the first lighthouse on the keys spelled the beginning of the end for the wrecking industry. Built in 1825, the Key West Lighthouse was destroyed by a hurricane just twenty-one years later. In 1852, the first of a series of specially designed lighthouses was erected in the keys. The new lighthouse had a skeletal tower made out of cast iron, which helped it withstand rough waves and winds.

Henry Flagler and the Overseas Railroad

By 1906, millionaire Henry Flagler had already built a railroad down the east coast of Florida. Flagler turned that coast into a winter haven for northern tourists by popularizing such resort towns as Palm Beach and Miami.

In 1906, Flagler began building a railroad over the water all the way to Key West. The task was an enormous one. It would take thousands of workers six years to build the bridges, tracks, and trestles that connected the keys to the mainland. By the following year, 2,500 workers were earning about $1.25 a day building Flagler's railroad.

The old railroad bridge that linked the Florida Keys to the mainland is shown in the foreground. The automobile bridge in use today can be seen behind it.

As the workers built the railway, they also created communities along the lines. One railway community was Marathon on Key Vaca. Marathon served as a base camp for the thousands of workers. It had dormitories, a hospital, a power plant, and basketball courts. The town's population plummeted after the workers went on to the next site.

Railroad building could be a dangerous occupation. In October 1906, a hurricane overturned a houseboat full of workers. The boat was swept out to sea, taking more than 160 workers with it. Only about seventy people were pulled from the stormy waters. More than 500 railroad workers died during the six-year project.

The Overseas Railroad was finally completed in 1912. In January of that year, Flagler made the trip through the keys in his private railroad car. The railroad quickly made the keys a vacation destination for millions of American tourists. Between 1912 and 1935, about 50 million passengers rode the train.

The Overseas Railroad operated until September 1935. That month, the disastrous Labor Day Hurricane devastated Flagler's railroad. The railway was sold to the State of Florida, which decided to create a roadway instead.

Tourism Today

Today, the main industry of the Florida Keys is tourism. Beginning in the 1970s, people from across the nation flocked to the keys. They came to explore the beautiful coral reefs, experience the excellent sport fishing, and enjoy the relaxed, laid-back way of life.

The keys are crowded with resorts to house the 4 million tourists who visit each year. Many of the visitors stay on Key Largo, the "diving capital of the world." Key Largo is home to John Pennekamp Coral Reef State Park. This underwater park includes one of the oldest reefs in the world. Visitors can dive, snorkel, or ride in glass-bottomed boats to view the reef's colorful fish and coral.

As more people discover the beauty of the keys and southern Florida, the threats to this fragile environment increase. Development increases the amount of pollutants in the waters around the keys. The reefs are also harmed when boats run aground on them or visitors touch or break off pieces of coral as souvenirs.

To protect this one-of-a-kind region, nearly twenty national or state conservation areas have been created. One of the largest is the Florida Keys National Marine Sanctuary. Created in 1990, the sanctuary protects more than 3,600 square miles (9,360 square kilometers) of ocean surrounding the keys. Oil and gas drilling are forbidden in the sanctuary, and large freighters must stay away, too. Fishing, boating, and other recreational activities are limited.

SANCTUARY FOR ARTISTS

Famous writers seem to be drawn to the keys. Here's a look at some of the famous authors who found inspiration in the keys.

Author Zane Grey hoists his catch, demonstrating why Long Key was such a popular vacation spot.

Zane Grey, who was famous for writing Westerns, began vacationing in Long Key in 1910. Grey was an avid sports fisher who served as president of the Long Key Fishing Club. While staying in the keys, Grey wrote *Wild Horse Mesa* and *Code of the West.*

American novelist and short-story writer Ernest Hemingway is shown at his typewriter as he works on one of his most famous novels, For Whom the Bell Tolls.

Ernest Hemingway was a famous novelist who lived in Key West from 1928 to 1940. During his stay, Hemingway wrote such classics as *For Whom the Bell Tolls* and *Death in the Afternoon*. Today, Key West celebrates this well-known author during Hemingway Days. One of the highlights of the festival is the Ernest Hemingway lookalike contest.

American playwright Tennessee Williams is photographed at his typewriter.

Tennessee Williams was a playwright who discovered Key West in the 1950s. Until his death in 1983, the author of *A Streetcar Named Desire* and *The Glass Menagerie* was a frequent visitor. A fine-arts center in the city is named after Williams.

Fifteen hundred runners cross the Seven Mile Bridge. The annual run across the longest of forty-three highway bridges in the Keys has become one of the most popular running events in the Southeast.

• Fast Fact •

There are more than forty bridges throughout the keys. The longest is Seven Mile Bridge, which connects Key Vaca and Sunshine Key; obviously, the bridge is 7 miles (11.2 kilometers) long. Long Key Bridge, which connects Long Key with Conch Key, is the second longest. It is 2.3 miles (3.7 kilometers) long.

Gulf of
Mexico

6

The Gulf of Mexico is a western arm of the Atlantic Ocean. It serves as the southern border of three Southeastern states— Louisiana, Mississippi, and Alabama. It also serves as the southwestern border of Florida. The gulf is connected to the Atlantic Ocean by the Florida Straits.

From the earliest days of European colonization in the Southeast, the gulf coast has played an important part in the settling and economic growth of the region. Over the past 400 years, the land along the gulf coast has changed hands many times. It belonged to the Spanish, the French, the British, and finally, the United States.

The gulf coast of the United States has a subtropical climate, with mild winters and very hot summers. The coast's sandy, white beaches and warm winter weather have attracted tourists and retirees since the mid-1800s. Hurricanes in the late summer and early fall are a threat along the coast.

WHAT'S IN A NAME?

Native American place names still abound in the Southeast. Here are just a few.

Alabama—from the Alibamon tribe, whose name meant "plant gatherers"

Biloxi—"first people"

Mississippi—"big river"

Pascagoula—"bread eaters"

Pensacola—"long-haired people"

Tampa—"lightning"

GULF FACTS

- The Gulf of Mexico covers about 700,000 square miles (1.82 million square kilometers).
- The Mississippi and the Rio Grande are two of the major rivers that empty into the gulf.
- The gulf shoreline measures about 3,000 miles (4,800 kilometers).
- The Gulf Stream, a current that runs through the Gulf of Mexico, affects weather all along the Atlantic coast of the United States.

Settlement

The first people to live along the gulf coast in the Southeast settled there about 10,000 years ago. Centuries later, before the first Europeans arrived, thousands of Native Americans lived along the gulf shores, including the Chickasaw, Choctaw, Biloxi, Apalachee, Pascagoula, Alabama, and Mobile tribes.

The native peoples of this area grew such crops as corn, squash, and beans. They also took fish and shellfish—including clams, oysters, and shrimps—from the gulf waters. In several areas along the gulf coast, native people created large *middens*, heaps of discarded shells and bones. One prehistoric trash heap was built by the Calusa people thousands of years ago in Osprey, Florida. The big shell mound is more than 12 feet (3.6 meters) high.

European Arrivals

The first Europeans to arrive in the gulf coast area were the Spanish. The earliest arrival was Juan Ponce de León, who briefly landed on Florida's west coast in 1513. Searching for a fountain of youth, Ponce de León found instead hostile Native Americans. He was attacked and mortally wounded. Other Spanish adventurers soon followed, including Alonso Álvarez de Piñeda (pih-NYAY-dah), who discovered Mobile Bay in Alabama in 1519. Perhaps the most famous Spaniard to explore the gulf coast was Hernando de Soto. De Soto began his unsuccessful quest for gold in the New World near Tampa Bay in 1539.

The first permanent Spanish settlement along the gulf coast was Pensacola, Florida. Pensacola was established in 1698. An attempt to found a Spanish colony on the same site more than 100 years earlier had ended in failure due to illness, bad weather, and native attacks.

The French were also interested in the gulf area, as well as the Mississippi River, which ran into the gulf. In 1682, René-Robert Cavelier (kav-ul-YAY), sieur de (lord of) La Salle, left Montreal, Canada, on a journey that would eventually take him down the Mississippi to the Gulf of Mexico. He claimed a huge area of land for France, naming it the Louisiana Territory after King Louis XIV of France.

The first French colony in the gulf region was Fort Maurepas (MO-ra-pah), settled in 1699 by two brothers, Pierre Le Moyne, sieur d'Iberville, and Jean Baptiste Le Moyne, sieur de Bienville. Fort Maurepas, the first capital of the Louisiana Territory, was located near what is now Ocean Springs, Mississippi. The brothers recognized the importance of the Mississippi as a major trade route in the colonies. By founding a colony near the mouth of the Mississippi, the French hoped to keep Spain and England off the river.

WHO'S GOT THE GULF?

Over the years, control of the gulf coast switched hands often. Here's a history of who was in control of the area at different times.

1513 Juan Ponce de León claims the territory of Florida for Spain.

1682 René-Robert Cavelier, sieur de La Salle, claims the Louisiana Territory for France. For decades, Spain and France argue over where the new territory ends and where Florida begins.

1762 France cedes the Louisiana Territory to Spain.

1763 Spain cedes its Florida territory to England.

1781 Spain retakes Florida.

1800 Spain cedes the Louisiana Territory to France.

1803 France sells the Louisiana Territory to the United States for the equivalent of four cents an acre (0.4 hectares). Known as the Louisiana Purchase, the sale doubles the size of the United States.

1821 Spain cedes Florida to the United States.

Migration Patterns

In the mid-1700s, an event taking place in Canada had a big effect on the southern Louisiana area of the gulf coast. In 1755, thousands of French settlers, known as Arcadians, were driven out of Nova Scotia by the British. About 4,000 Arcadians, or Cajuns, as they became known, traveled to southern Louisiana. They joined French settlers who had already made homes in the area.

The Cajuns settled along the waterways and bayous of the gulf coastal area. In the most isolated spots, Cajuns were able to hold on to their unique (yoo-NEEK) culture, including the use of Cajun French. Cajun French is a dialect that uses English, Spanish, and Native American words. Cajun dishes, such as *jambalaya* and *gumbo*, as well as Cajun music called *zydeco*, still survive today.

While the Cajuns were settling into the gulf area, many Native American tribes in the area were being pushed out. As more settlers arrived in the region, they looked for the best, richest land on which to build homes, and native peoples were forced off land that had been theirs. However, some tribes refused to give up without a fight.

Beginning in 1817, the Seminoles in Florida waged war on white settlers and battled the U.S. government on and off until 1858. By 1842, however, most Native American tribes along the gulf coast had been forced north to the newly established Indian Territory in Oklahoma.

Commerce

In the early days of gulf coast colonization, farming and fishing were the two key industries of the area. Many settlers in the area were subsistence farmers: They grew just enough corn, soybeans, and other vegetables to get by. Some supplemented their diets and their incomes by hunting for deer pelts to trade and catching fish in the gulf waters.

Fishermen in the gulf took mackerel, bluefish, trout, crabs, oysters, clams, and shrimps from the waters. Today, the fishing industry remains a key part of the gulf coast's economy. Some important

fishing ports along the southeastern gulf coast include Biloxi, Mississippi; Panama City, Florida; and Pascagoula, Florida.

    Shipping and trade were also important from the earliest colonial days. Goods traveled down the Mississippi River to the gulf and then on to other markets in the colonies and in Europe. The river route to the gulf was the main shipping route of its time. Fur traders, as well as cotton and sugar plantation owners used the Mississippi to transport their wares to the gulf ports. Manufactured goods and other items from Europe and the colonies moved through gulf ports before being transported to trading posts and settlements up north.

    One major port during the 1800s was Apalachicola, Florida. By 1860, the transportation of cotton

Local surfers take advantage of 5-foot-high (1.5 meters) waves along the Gulf of Mexico before the arrival of Tropical Storm Dean.

SHARK ATTACKS

On July 6, 2001, eight-year-old Jessie Arbogast was swimming in the warm, shallow waters off the Gulf Coast of Florida. Suddenly, Jessie was attacked by a 7-foot (2.1-meter), 200-pound (90-kilogram) bull shark. The shark bit off the young boy's arm.

Jessie was rushed to a hospital, where doctors were able to reattach his arm. However, Jessie lost much of his blood during the attack. He suffered permanent damage that continues to affect him today.

Although the attack was horrifying, shark attacks are rare. Experts say that there are between fifty and seventy-five unprovoked shark attacks around the world each year. Few of these prove fatal.

How can swimmers lessen their chances of being attacked by a shark? Experts say to never swim alone, avoid bright swimwear and shiny jewelry, and pay attention to the water around you. One final fact to keep in mind: Dawn and dusk are the favorite feeding times of many shark species.

had helped Apalachicola become the third-largest port on the gulf. Mobile, Alabama, was another major cotton port. Today, two Mississippi cities, Gulfport and Pascagoula, are the two important deepwater ports in the gulf. Each year, thousands of ships pass through these ports, bringing cargo from all over the world.

In recent years, manufacturing has become important to many gulf towns. Gulfport, Mississippi, for example, is home to industries that produce metal goods and chemicals. Biloxi, Mississippi has factories that make boats and fishing equipment. Other coastal towns produce electronics, textiles, clothing, and machinery.

Tourism

Since the mid-1800s, the gulf coast's warm, sunny climate and beautiful beaches have made it a magnet for people living in the north. Over the years, many towns along the gulf have seen their populations skyrocket as tourists and retirees come to the area for sun and fun.

Many cities on the gulf are known for their vacation-friendly attitude. St. Petersburg, Florida, for example, is known as the Sunshine City, while Panama City has become a hot spot for college students on spring break. With its many resorts, floating casinos, and beautiful beaches, the gulf coast of Mississippi has earned a reputation as the Playground of the South.

HURRICANE COAST

The gulf coast has been hit with several severe hurricanes in recent history. Here are some of them.

Hurricane	Date	Location	Damage	Deaths
Audrey	June 1957	Louisiana, Mississippi	$150 million	390
Camille	August 1969	Mississippi, Alabama, Florida	$1.4 billion	256
Agnes	June 1972	Florida	$2.1 billion	122
Andrew	August 1992	Florida, Louisiana	$26.5 billion	26
Opal	October 1995	Florida, Alabama	$3 billion	37

War and the Gulf

In the early 1860s, the gulf coast's economy was thriving, thanks to shipping, fishing, and other industries. Then the Civil War (1861–1865) began. Louisiana, Mississippi, Alabama, and Florida joined the rest of the Southeastern states in seceding from the United States. In 1861, they joined the Confederate States of America under the leadership of Mississippi politician Jefferson Davis.

JEFFERSON DAVIS, CONFEDERATE PRESIDENT

In 1861, Mississippi politician Jefferson Davis was chosen to head the new Confederate States of America. Before the war, Davis had served as a U.S. senator from Mississippi. He was also secretary of war under President Franklin Pierce. Davis was not in favor of the South seceding from the nation. When Mississippi seceded, however, Davis withdrew from the U.S. senate.

After the South's defeat, Davis was imprisoned by the United States for two years. Although he was indicted for treason, he was never tried. Beginning in 1878, Davis spent the final years of his life at Beauvoir, his gulf coast estate near Biloxi. He died in 1889 at the age of eighty-one.

The Union quickly began a blockade of Confederate ports. The blockade stretched along the gulf coast and up the Atlantic coast. Such important Confederate port cities as Biloxi, Mississippi; Mobile, Alabama; and Pensacola, Florida were seriously harmed by the blockade. People throughout the gulf region who counted on shipments of food, medicine, and other items suffered greatly during the war.

The Battle of Mobile Bay, the most important naval battle of the Civil War, took place in the Gulf of Mexico. In August 1864, Union captain David

Admiral David Farragut and his crew aboard the USS Pensacola in 1868. Farragut led Union forces aboard the Pensacola to victory in the battles of New Orleans and Mobile Bay during the Civil War.

Quartermaster Richard Knowles poses with his sword aboard a ship during the Civil War. Knowles is reported to have lashed Admiral Farragut to the rigging to keep him from blowing overboard during the battle of Mobile Bay.

Farragut sailed eighteen ships into Mobile Bay. Even though the bay was loaded with Confederate mines, Farragut pressed forward. "Damn the torpedoes!" he said. "Full speed ahead!" Farragut took the bay and cut off an important supply route for the Confederate army.

The Civil War devastated the economy of the gulf coast region as it did in all other Southeastern states. It wasn't until the 1940s and the outbreak of World War II (1939–1945) that the area began to rebound. During World War II, the gulf coast became a key site for air force and navy bases and training facilities, as well as shipbuilding and other war industries. The coast is still home to many military bases, and warships are still built here.

A GULF TOWN FOR RETIRED VETERANS

In 1910, Senator W.H. Lynn of New York decided to set aside a place in Florida for Northern Civil War veterans. Lynn placed notices in a veterans' journal, advertising more than 7,000 plots of land for sale. The result was the town of Lynn Haven. Lynn Haven is the only town in the Southeast—and the entire South—that has a Union war memorial.

The Gulf Today

Each year, more people are attracted to the gulf coast's beautiful sandy beaches. Those living along the coast have recognized the need to protect their shoreline. In order to preserve the beaches for future generations, some coastal officials are carefully regulating development in their communities.

Pollution can also cause problems along the gulf. Rivers that drain into the gulf sometimes dump

MARDI GRAS IN MOBILE

Mardi Gras, or Fat Tuesday, is held each year on the day before Ash Wednesday. Mardi Gras was begun in Europe during the Middle Ages as a way to celebrate before Lent. Lent is a Christian season of fasting before Easter that begins on Ash Wednesday. Mardi Gras is a time for parades and parties.

One of many colorfully decorated floats winds its way through the streets of New Orleans during the annual Mardi Gras celebration.

New Orleans is famous for its Mardi Gras festivities—but the very first Fat Tuesday celebration in the United States was held in Mobile, Alabama! French settlers in Mobile celebrated the first Mardi Gras in 1703, just one year after the town had been founded. They brought the carnival tradition, which dates from medieval times, from their homeland. The first Mardi Gras in the New World probably included a large feast, but not the parades that revelers enjoy today.

chemicals, fertilizers, and other harmful materials into the water. In places where there is oil drilling, the possibility of an oil spill is cause for concern. People along the coast are working to make sure that the Gulf of Mexico stays as healthy as possible.

In 1971, 150 miles (240 kilometers) of the gulf coast from Mississippi to Florida were set aside as the Gulf Islands National Seashore. Visitors to the seashore can see ancient middens, the shell mounds that served as trash heaps for early Native Americans.

• Fast Fact •

The world's longest human-made beach is Harrison County Sand Beach on Mississippi's gulf coast. It is 26 miles (41.6 kilometers) long.

Mississippi
River

7

The Mississippi River is the nation's most important waterway. The river played a key role in the development of our nation, both economically and socially. For thousands of years, people have used the river as a means of exploration and transportation. Settlers used the river and its tributaries to travel from the eastern United States to the west.

The Mississippi has its source in Lake Itasca in northwest Minnesota. From there, it winds its way past ten states to the Mississippi Delta in the Gulf of Mexico. The delta is a large area of land formed by the buildup of sand, soil, and other river deposits. In all, the river travels 2,348 miles (3,757 kilometers), twisting and turning all the way.

The lower Mississippi runs past five Southeastern states. It enters the Southeast on the lower western border of Kentucky. The river marks the western boundaries of Tennessee and Mississippi. It also serves as the eastern border of Arkansas and upper Louisiana, finally cutting through the bottom of the state until it empties into the Gulf of Mexico.

More than 250 *tributaries*, smaller rivers or streams, flow into the Mississippi. The chief tributaries that pass through the Southeast are the Ohio, Arkansas, and Red Rivers. The Mississippi drains more than 1.2 million square miles (3.12 million square kilometers) between the Rockies and the Alleghenies, carrying rainwater and melted snow to the Gulf of Mexico.

Settlement

The Mississippi was formed about 10,000 years ago after the last Ice Age. Melting glaciers carved the twisting, turning channels that would become the big river and its many tributaries. Soon after, humans settled around the river. One group of early native people was known as the Mound Builders. These people used large dirt mounds as burial and ceremonial sites. The Mound Builders disappeared about 100 years before the first Europeans arrived in the area.

When the Europeans began arriving along the lower Mississippi, several different Native American tribes lived along the riverbanks. These tribes included the Natchez, Choctaw, Creek, Chickasaw, and Quapaw. The tribes planted crops of beans, corn, and squash. They also hunted in the forests along the river and fished in its waters.

WHAT'S IT CALLED?

Over the centuries, the Mississippi River has had many names. Native Americans in the area called it *messipi*, meaning "big water," and *mee-zee-see-bee*, meaning "father of the waters." Hernando de Soto named it Rio Espiritu Santo. The French called it the River St. Louis and the River Colbert. Because of its brown appearance, the river today is sometimes known by its nickname: Big Muddy.

European Exploration

The first European to see the inland Mississippi was Spanish explorer Hernando de Soto in 1541. De Soto traveled throughout the Southeast, searching unsuccessfully for gold. The cruel conquistador died in the New World. De Soto's men sank his body in the Mississippi River so that area natives would not learn of his death. The natives thought that de Soto was a god—if they had found out that the "god" was mortal, they might have attacked the remaining men.

More than 130 years after de Soto, the French arrived. The first were Father Jacques Marquette and Louis Joliet in 1673. Nine years later, Réné Robert Cavelier (kav-ul-YAY), sieur de La Salle, journeyed from St. Louis, Missouri, to the big river's mouth in the Gulf of Mexico. La Salle claimed the entire region for France, naming it Louisiana after the French king Louis XIV.

The French were the first Europeans to settle in the area. They set up trading posts and fortresses along the river's banks. These tiny outposts in the Southeast would eventually grow to be some of the region's biggest, most important cities. One of the earliest French settlements was Fort Rosalie, founded in 1716. It later grew to be the port city of Natchez, Mississippi.

The French settled another important Mississippi River town in 1718: New Orleans. Strategically located near the mouth of the river, New Orleans was named capital of the Louisiana territory in 1722. By 1840, it was the nation's second most important port and one of the nation's largest cities. Other important river towns that started as French forts or trading posts are Memphis, Tennessee, and Baton Rouge, Louisiana.

In 1760, Great Britain gained control of all land east of the Mississippi. Soon, settlers from the east were using the river and its tributaries as roadways to settlement. After the American Revolution (1775–1783), the United States took control of the formerly British land. In 1803, President Thomas Jefferson bought the huge area west of the river that belonged to France. The Louisiana Purchase, as the sale is known, doubled the size of the United States and ended all foreign control of the Mississippi.

La Salle claims Louisiana for France in this painting by J.N. Marchand.

Commerce and Travel

One of the earliest industries practiced along the banks of the Mississippi was agriculture. The river's floodplains ensured rich, fertile farmland for all who settled in the area. Some early settlers in the area brought African slaves with them from the eastern colonies. Before long, large cotton, sugar, and rice plantations dotted the riverbanks. By the 1860s, the system of slavery was firmly in place along the Mississippi.

One of the most important centers of plantation life was Baton Rouge. Large cotton plantations and a riverside location helped the town grow into an important Mississippi port. In 1849, the thriving city replaced New Orleans as the capital of Louisiana. Other important cotton ports included Memphis and Natchez, as well as Vicksburg, Mississippi.

Farther south along the river, sugar plantations drove the economy. The first sugar plantation was established in the New Orleans area in the late 1600s. At first, the sugarcane was used mainly to make rum. Then in 1794, a plantation owner found a way to granulate sugar. Growing sugarcane quickly became a profitable industry.

THE NATCHEZ REVOLT

Early French settlers along the Mississippi River generally got along well with the Native American tribes who lived in the area. The French traded guns, tools, and liquor with the natives for furs and other goods. In 1729, however, the French alienated the Natchez, the most powerful tribe in the area. The French wanted to take some of the tribe's best land along the river. The furious Natchez attacked Fort Rosalie, destroying the settlement and killing the French commander there. French settlers retaliated by nearly wiping out the Natchez tribe.

An Important Trade Route

From the earliest days, the Mississippi provided farmers, traders, and merchants with an excellent means of transportation to get their goods to market.

The earliest trade along the river was in furs. Later, timber, tobacco, cotton, corn, wheat, and other items traveled along the big river on their way to their final destinations.

The first people to travel the Mississippi had been Native Americans using handcrafted bark canoes. Early settlers modified the design of the canoes, making them larger in order to carry loads of furs and other trade items. Canoes also served as the first ferries, carrying Native Americans and settlers from one bank of the river to the other. Later ferries included rowboats and rafts, often guided by ropes strung between the two banks.

As the need for bigger boats arose, flatboats came into use along the Mississippi. These bargelike craft could be floated down the river with the currents as far as New Orleans. Unfortunately, there was no way for the flatboats to get back up the river, so the big barges were chopped up and sold for timber. Then a flatboat crew could follow the Natchez Trace from Natchez, Mississippi, as far north as Memphis, Tennessee. The Natchez Trace was a rough, dangerous trail that had first served as a migration route for buffalo and other animals and later as a hunting path for natives. Settlers traveling the trace had to face wild animals, poisonous snakes, and roadside robbers.

Keelboats, which could navigate both down and up the river, were an

YELLOW FEVER ON THE MISSISSIPPI

In the eighteenth and nineteenth centuries, the low-lying, swampy coastlines along parts of the Mississippi were breeding grounds for mosquitoes. Some mosquitoes carried *yellow fever*, a virus that caused fever, nausea, organ damage, and death. Outbreaks of the disease were common along the Mississippi. In 1853, for example, more than 7,800 people died during an epidemic in New Orleans. In 1878, yellow fever decimated the population of Memphis, Tennessee. Although a vaccine now exists to prevent yellow fever, there is still no way to treat the disease once it has been caught.

improvement over the flatboats. These large vessels were propelled by long poles or hauled up the river by men pulling towropes along the riverbanks. During the days of the keelboats, a trip from Pittsburgh, Pennsylvania, to New Orleans might take only three weeks, while the return trip could take four months or more. In the 1810s, steamboats replaced keelboats as the preferred method of river travel.

Today, more than 400 million tons (360 million metric tons) of freight are transported on the Mississippi each year, making it the most important inland waterway in the United States. Chemicals, timber, steel, grain, and oil are all carried down the Mississippi to the Gulf of Mexico and, from there, all over the world. Coal, fertilizer, food, and manufactured goods are all carried upstream. Four of the ten busiest U.S. ports are located along the Mississippi River in Louisiana: South Louisiana, New Orleans, Baton Rouge, and Plaquemines.

MIKE FINK, KEELBOATER

Mississippi keelboaters were known to be a hard-working, hard-drinking group. One of the most famous keelboaters was Mike Fink, who worked the river beginning around 1790. Fink, an excellent navigator, fighter, and rifleman, was also quite boastful. After Fink's death in 1823, tall tales that the boatman had created about himself were told and retold. He is one of America's earliest folk heroes.

Steamboats on the River

In 1811, the steamboat *New Orleans* chugged down the Mississippi, the first such boat on the river. This event marked a new era in riverboat transportation. Soon, steamboats became the number one way to transport goods up- and downstream. Steamboats were quicker and cheaper than flatboats and keelboats.

For those who wished to travel from one river town to another, steamboats were much more

comfortable than the land route via wagons and stagecoaches. Steamboat owners quickly turned their attention to providing luxury accommodations for river travelers. To attract business, they began decorating their "floating palaces" with crystal chandeliers, hand-carved furniture, carpeting, china, and silver.

The steamboats were used not only for trade and travel, but also for fun. The first "showboat" plied the waters of the Mississippi in 1817. These floating theaters brought music, magic, and other types of entertainment to people living along the banks of the river. One of the largest showboats of the day had a stage, a wax museum, and stalls for forty horses. The showboats were important until the early 1900s, when automobiles and motion pictures put them out of business.

Despite the convenience and comfort of steamboats, there were some serious problems. During the summer, when the water was low, the big boats were forced to remain tied up at the docks. Travel by steamboat could also be dangerous. Snags, sandbars, accidents, and explosions caused the sinking of hundreds of steamboats. By 1852, there had been nearly 1,000 steamboat accidents on the river.

The steamboat era didn't last long. Beginning in the 1870s, railroads began competing with the ships. Soon, the faster, cheaper trains had made steamboats obsolete. By 1910, barges and diesel-powered towboats had replaced the old steamboats to haul goods up and down the river.

THE SULTANA DISASTER

The worst steamboat disaster in history occurred on the lower Mississippi in 1865. On April 26, the *Sultana* set off from Vicksburg, Mississippi. On board were more than 2,000 Union soldiers who had just been released from Confederate prisons. In the early morning hours, as the ship sailed past Memphis, Tennessee, one of its boilers exploded. The ship burned and sank. About 1,700 men lost their lives in the disaster.

War Comes to the Mississippi

During the Civil War (1861–1865), the Union recognized the importance of the Mississippi River to the Confederate cause. If Union troops could take control of the Mississippi, they would be able to separate the South from the western slaveholding states, as well as from its source of supplies. Because of the Union's naval blockade from the Gulf of Mexico to the Atlantic coast, trade on the Mississippi ceased during the war, but the big river became a major pathway for moving troops.

In April 1862, Union captain David Farragut took control of New Orleans. From there, Union troops moved up the Mississippi, capturing port after port, including Baton Rouge, Louisiana, and Natchez. Meanwhile, Union troops worked their way south along the river. They took control of Memphis and eventually Vicksburg, an important Confederate supply port. Total Union control of the Mississippi was an important milestone of the Civil War.

THE BATTLE OF VICKSBURG

In early 1863, Vicksburg was the last important Mississippi port city still under Confederate control. In April, Union general Ulysses S. Grant laid siege to the city. At first, Grant tried to attack Vicksburg from the river. When this failed, he and his troops circled around the city. A second attack, this time by land, was again unsuccessful.

Grant and his soldiers settled in, determined to starve Vicksburg into surrender. Residents hid in caves that they had dug into the hillside while Union troops bombarded the city with cannon and gunfire. Finally, after forty-seven days without supplies, starving Confederates were forced to surrender. The battle marked total Union control of the Mississippi River.

opposite:
Barges are backed up along the banks of the Mississippi. The riverbanks can barely be seen because they are submerged due to extensive flooding.

The Civil War ruined the economy of the Southeastern states and the cities located along the Mississippi. Before the war, the Mississippi port cities had been rich and important. After the war, many were devastated and destroyed, as were cities in other parts of the Southeast.

Some Mississippi port cities became the scenes of segregation, discrimination, and racial violence. In 1866, for example, a race riot in New Orleans left forty-eight people dead, most of them black. That same year, Memphis also experienced a race riot.

In 1892, a New Orleans court case paved the way for legal segregation in the South for decades to come. That year, a black man named Homer Plessy challenged New Orleans's "black codes," laws that segregated blacks and whites. Plessy's case, called *Plessy v. Ferguson,* was appealed all the way to the Supreme Court of the United States. In 1896, the Supreme Court made what many historians feel was one of the worst decisions in its history. The justices decreed that the black codes were legal. For more than fifty years, "separate but equal" would be the way of the Southeast until the civil rights movement in the 1950s.

Flooding along the Lower Mississippi

Flooding is a serious problem along the lower Mississippi River. Ever since people settled in the area, deadly floods have endangered homes, farms, livestock, and humans. During the worst floods, the river has risen as much as 50 feet (15 meters) above normal levels.

In April 1927, the worst flood in the history of the lower Mississippi wreaked havoc throughout the region. Heavy rains caused the Mississippi to overflow its banks, flooding the homes of nearly 1 million people. Greenville, Mississippi was underwater for

more than two months. The Great Mississippi Flood caused the deaths of as many as 1,000 people and ruined more than 5 million acres (2 million hectares) of farmland. It is considered one of the worst natural disasters in U.S. history.

After the 1927 flood, the U.S. government began looking for ways to prevent such a disaster from ever happening again. Nearly 1,600 miles (2,560 kilometers) of levees were constructed along the lower Mississippi. A *levee* is a high bank that is built to prevent a river from overflowing. In addition, floodways and spillways were also built. These artificially constructed channels divert floodwaters away from the river. In New Orleans, for example, a spillway diverts water into the Gulf of Mexico.

• Fast Fact •

The earliest known attempts at flood control along the lower Mississippi took place in 1727. That year, a levee, or bank, 36 miles (57.6 kilometers) long was built to protect New Orleans from flooding.

Although steps have been taken to lessen the damage caused by flooding along the lower Mississippi, there is no way to prevent floods from occurring. Recent floods in the area took place in 1973, 1983, and 1997.

The Mississippi Today

Today, the Mississippi continues to be the most important inland waterway in the United States. Oil tankers and barges, as well as tourist boats, ply the waters, carrying everything from petroleum and oil to wheat and rice. Because of its standing as an important trade area, the Mississippi has attracted numerous industries over the years. Agriculture continues to be a key part of the river economy.

As the Mississippi area becomes more crowded, increased pollution threatens the river. Sewage,

opposite:
W.C. Handy is shown playing the trumpet at age seventy-six in 1949. Handy is known as the Father of the Blues.

MISSISSIPPI MUSIC

The Mississippi Delta is known as the birthplace of the blues. The blues began when slaves in the cotton fields put their troubles into musical form. Memphis, Tennessee is one Southeastern city that has an especially rich musical heritage. W.C. Handy, known as the Father of the Blues, wrote his first blues song in Memphis in 1909. Other blues musicians who got their start in Memphis include Howlin' Wolf, Alberta Hunter, and B.B. King. In 1953, another musical milestone occurred in Memphis when Elvis Presley, the future King of Rock and Roll, recorded his first record.

fertilizer runoff, and chemicals from riverside factories are all causes of concern along the river today. Another serious problem is the decreasing amount of wetlands along the river. As wetlands disappear, native plants and animals are also in danger of disappearing. Spillways and levees, while important in reducing flood damage, have also reduced *sedimentation*, river deposits that keep wetlands healthy. In 1990, the Breaux Act was passed to restore and protect river wetlands and marshes. Local, regional, and federal groups are looking at ways to balance flood protection with environmental concerns.

Ouachita Mountains

8

The Ouachita (WASH-ih-taw) Mountains are a range of peaks and ridges that extend more than 200 miles (320 kilometers) from central Arkansas into southeast Oklahoma. The range is one of the few in the United States that runs east to west; most mountain ranges in the nation run north to south. The highest point in the Southeast section of the range is Magazine Point, which is 2,753 feet (826 meters) high.

The area around the mountains is known for its unique terrain and natural beauty. Much of the Ouachitas lies within Ouachita National Forest. Hot Springs National Park is in the foothills. This park, located on a *fault*, or break in the Earth's crust, is famous for its warm mineral springs. Heat from deep within Earth warms spring waters to temperatures that average 143 degrees Fahrenheit (62 degrees Celsius).

• Fast Fact •

The word Ouachita comes from the Native American term *washitah*, **meaning "good hunting grounds."**

The Spanish explorer Hernando de Soto (1499–1542), who was the first European to discover the Mississippi River in 1540.

Settlement

The first humans in the Ouachita area arrived about 10,000 years ago. These ancestors of later Native American tribes lived and hunted in the Ouachita valleys. Later groups *quarried*, or dug, novaculite and quartz to make arrowheads and tools. *Novaculite* is a hard, dense mineral that is white or gray in color. Today, it is used to make abrasive cleansers and whetstones (knife sharpeners).

Before Europeans arrived in the area, such tribes as the Quapaw, Caddo, and Cherokee (CHAYR-uh-key) settled in the fertile foothills of the Ouachitas. These groups grew corn, beans, and squash and raised chicken and other livestock. They lived in the area until they were forced to move to the Indian Territory (now Oklahoma) in the early 1800s.

Native American tribes knew about the hot springs in the Ouachitas. They may have told early European explorers and settlers about the springs' healing powers. The first European to see the springs was probably the Spanish adventurer Hernando de Soto in 1541. De Soto was followed by French explorers in the 1600s.

The first settlements in the area were started in the early 1800s. Settlers were attracted to the Ouachitas by the mineral and timber wealth of the area. They also farmed in the fertile foothills and valleys at the mountain base. At first, few people settled in the upland areas. The most famous settlement in the Ouachita area, Hot Springs, was established in 1807.

Commerce

One of the earliest and most important industries in the Ouachitas was mining. Beginning in the 1800s, miners took minerals, metals, and gemstones out of the mountains. The most plentiful substance in the area is quartz.

Quartz mining in the Ouachitas became very important during World War II (1939–1945), when quartz was used in military communication equipment. In 1943, more than 212,000 pounds (95,400 kilograms) of quartz were taken out of the Ouachitas for military use. Today, there are still dozens of small quartz mines in the area.

The area is also home to the only diamond mine in North America, located in Murfreesboro, Arkansas. Diamonds were first discovered here in 1906. Most of the diamonds found there have been small. Over the years, however, some big finds have been made. The largest diamond ever mined in the area was 40.23 carats uncut.

The 80-acre (32-hectare) site is now preserved as Crater of Diamonds State Park. Visitors can mine the area for diamonds—and keep whatever they find! Since 1972, more than 22,000 diamonds have been taken from the land.

These visitors to Crater of Diamonds State Park use a shovel and sieve to search for diamonds.

A MECCA FOR MINERS

The Ouachita Mountains are known for their wealth of minerals, metals, and gems. Here is a list of some the items that have been dug out of the mountains.

Metals	Gemstones	Natural Fuels
aluminum	agate	coal
copper	amethyst	natural gas
lead	diamond	petroleum
manganese	garnet	
mercury	jasper	
silver	quartz	
titanium	turquoise	
zinc		

Tourism

As early as the 1800s, people journeyed to the hot springs of the Ouachitas to try to cure themselves of various ailments, from arthritis, rheumatism, and skin diseases to heart, liver, and kidney problems. In 1832, the federal government set aside the area as Hot Springs Reservation. In 1921, the area was designated a national park. "Taking the cure" in the waters remained a popular treatment until the invention of antibiotics to treat various illnesses.

Beginning in the 1920s, the Hot Springs area attracted a different kind of attention. Gangsters from New York took an interest in the small town. They built casinos, bordellos, and betting parlors. Soon, crime bosses like Al "Scarface" Capone and Charles "Lucky" Luciano were giving the tiny Arkansas town a reputation as the vacation destination for the underworld. The gangster era finally came to a close in the 1960s, when the casinos and other illegal establishments were shut down.

Owney Madden (left) leaves Sing Sing Prison with a friend in 1933. Madden was known as New York's Public Enemy No. 2.

THE BOSS OF HOT SPRINGS

Owen "Owney the Killer" Madden (1892–1964) was a bootlegger, murderer, and gang boss in New York. After migrating from England as a boy, Madden became the leader of the Gopher Gang. This group of thugs terrorized Hell's Kitchen on New York's West Side. By the age of twenty-one, the bad Brit had been arrested more than forty times. In the 1920s and 1930s, Madden worked with some of the most notorious gangsters in New York, including "Dutch" Schultz, "Lucky" Luciano, and Meyer Lansky. Madden even owned part of the Cotton Club, a famous nightclub in Harlem where alcohol was sold illegally. In the mid-1930s, Madden retired from the New York crime scene and moved his base of operations to Hot Springs.

Today

Today, the Ouachita Mountains are the top tourist attraction in Arkansas. At 9 square miles (23.4 square kilometers), Hot Springs National Park is the smallest national park in the United States. Each year, 1.5 million visitors come to the park to visit its bathhouses. Although only one of the historic bathhouses, Buckstaff Bathhouse, is still in operation today, the restored buildings themselves are a reminder of times past.

Another attraction in the mountains is Ouachita National Forest, the largest and oldest such park in the Southeast. This national forest is a paradise of rivers, wilderness areas, mountains, lakes, and trails. Lake Ouachita, in that area, is the largest artificial lake in Arkansas.

The Winding Stairs area of the Little Missouri River in the Ouachita Mountains of Arkansas is one of the area's many natural attractions.

GETTING A SHOWER UNDER THE ARTESIAN GUSHER, ARBORDALE-FOUNTAIN LAKE.

HOT SPRINGS NATIONAL PARK, ARK.

FASCINATING FACTS
ABOUT THE HOT SPRINGS

- The hot springs discharge more than 750,000 gallons (2.85 million liters) of water each day.

- There are forty-seven different mineral springs in Hot Springs.

- Each hot spring has its own name, such as Magnesia, Arsenic, Mud, and Big Iron. Two cold water springs in the area that dried up were known as Kidney and Liver.

- The first bathhouses in Hot Springs were built in the 1830s. These brush huts and log cabins were constructed directly over the springs.

- Water in the hot springs is rainwater that fell about 4,000 years ago. It took thousands of years for the rainwater to seep deep below Earth's surface. However, it took only a year or two for the superheated water to shoot back up to the surface.

- No one knows how long the hot springs will continue to flow.

THE BOY FROM HOT SPRINGS

William Jefferson Clinton, our forty-second president, was born in Hope, Arkansas, in 1946, but he was raised in Hot Springs. From the age of six, Clinton lived, learned, and played in the booming little city. He left Hot Springs in 1964 after graduating from high school. In 1979, thirty-two-year-old Clinton, a Democrat, became the youngest governor ever elected in Arkansas. In 1992, he was elected president of the United States.

Shenandoah
River and Valley

9

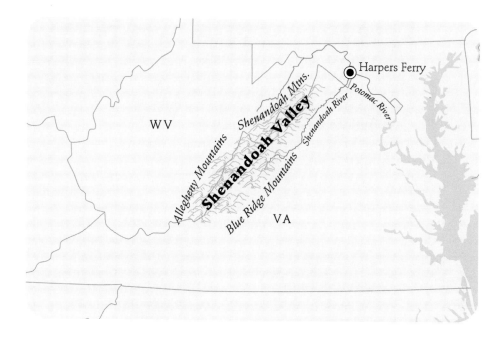

The Shenandoah River is a winding, twisting waterway in northern Virginia. It flows through and drains the Shenandoah Valley, a 200-mile-long (320-kilometer-long) valley situated between the Blue Ridge and Allegheny Mountains in the Appalachians. The river has two forks at its southern end: the North Fork and the South Fork. It forms a main branch at Riverton, Virginia, where the two forks meet. From Riverton, the Shenandoah flows northeast, meeting the Potomac River at Harpers Ferry in West Virginia. The Shenandoah is shallow and not navigable.

• Fast Fact •

Shenandoah **is a native word that may mean "daughter of the stars," "big meadow," or "river through the spruces."**

The Shenandoah area is home to some of the richest farmland in the United States. Since the 1700s, settlers have taken advantage of the fertile soil around the river. The Shenandoah Valley's role as a major food supplier for the Confederate Army made it the focus of many battles during the Civil War (1861–1865).

Settlement

Thousands of years ago, the Shenandoah Valley area was settled by the ancestors of later Native Americans. These earliest Americans grew crops of squash, beans, and corn. Later Native American tribes used the valley as hunting grounds. Such tribes as the Shawnee, Iroquois (EE-ra-kwoy), and Monocan hunted buffalo, elk, deer, and other wildlife. At times, the tribes burned the valley to make sure that the area remained treeless and grassy. This good grazing land attracted the big game that the tribes liked to hunt.

The first Europeans to explore the valley may have been Spanish missionaries as early as the 1630s. The first known explorer, however, was a German doctor named John Lederer. He took careful notes during his trips through the valley from the 1660s to the 1710s. His writings encouraged others to visit and settle in the area.

In 1716, Virginia's governor, Alexander Spotswood, claimed the area for Great Britain. He began selling parcels of land to British settlers. He wanted to make sure that the area was kept out of the hands of rival French settlers.

The Shenandoah area quickly attracted settlers from the North. The river was filled with many kinds of fish, and the forests teemed with deer, elk, turkeys, and other wildlife. Even in years when crops failed, people could turn to the rivers and forests for survival. Some early settlers were Germans and Dutch from the Pennsylvania area, who started arriving as early as 1726. Beginning in 1732, Scotch-Irish and English settlers from the Virginia coast also made their homes there.

The Shenandoah Valley served as an important pathway to the rugged lands to the west. As more people settled along the Atlantic coast, land there became expensive and hard to obtain. Settlers looked to the west as a place to gain land of their own. In the

1800s, thousands of people from Pennsylvania and the Atlantic coast made their way through the Shenandoah Valley. Abraham Lincoln's family was just one of the groups of settlers who traveled through the Shenandoah Valley on their way westward.

Economy

One of the earliest and most important industries in the Shenandoah area was agriculture. Since the early 1700s, residents of this fertile farming area have grown apples, hay, grains, and other produce. The valley soon became known as a "breadbasket" of the south because it was the source of food for a large area.

Livestock and dairy farms were also important to the Shenandoah economy. Valley farmers raised sheep, poultry, and cows on farms throughout the region. Agriculture continues to be an important part of the Shenandoah economy today.

Many early businesses in the valley revolved around agriculture. Mills for grinding grain, cider presses, and tanneries all developed as a result of the area's farming economy. Other industries made use of the region's other natural resources. Lumber and mining were two such businesses in the Shenandoah region.

The Civil War

The Shenandoah Valley played a major role in the Civil War. At the northern end of the valley lies Washington, D.C., capital of the Union. The valley provided a pathway to the capital for the South. For the North, the Shenandoah Valley represented an important source of food for the Southeastern states—and the Confederate army. The North knew that control of the valley meant control of a vital source of Confederate supplies. Because of the valley's strategic location, many battles were fought there.

HARPERS FERRY

Harpers Ferry, West Virginia is located at the junction of the Shenandoah and Potomac Rivers. The town was first settled in 1732. In 1747, it gained its name after Robert Harper began a ferry service across the rivers. In 1796, Harpers Ferry became an important center for arms production. Many of the rifles used in the Civil War (1861–1865) were made there.

In 1859, Harpers Ferry was the site of an important antislavery event. In October, abolitionist John Brown and eighteen supporters seized the U.S. weapons storehouse in the town. (*Abolitionists* were people against slavery.) Brown hoped to start a slave rebellion and create a haven for blacks in what is now West Virginia. Robert E. Lee, then a colonel in the U.S. Army, attacked the arsenal, and fourteen of Brown's men were killed. Brown was captured and found guilty of murder and treason. He was executed by hanging on December 2, 1859.

Southerners were furious about Brown's violent attack on their way of life. Many Northerners, however, looked upon Brown as a hero for the antislavery cause. A popular song of the time declared that "John Brown's body lies a-mouldering in the grave," but his "soul goes marching on."

War in the Valley

Confederate general Thomas "Stonewall" Jackson began his Valley Campaign in March 1862. Over the next few months, Jackson and his troops defeated Northern troops that greatly outnumbered their own. One town, Winchester, changed hands more than seventy times. About 8,000 Civil War dead are buried near the town.

During the Civil War, life in the Shenandoah Valley changed drastically. Residents in the area opened their homes as hospitals to soldiers of both sides. Other families found their homes taken over to serve as headquarters for Confederate and Union troops. Much of the area's food and other supplies were used to feed the thousands of troops that marched up and down the valley.

In May 1864, life for people of the valley took a turn for the worse when Union general Philip Henry Sheridan arrived. Sheridan's mission was to take control of the valley and destroy the Confederate breadbasket. In September, Sheridan and his troops took on General Jubal Early's men in the Battle of Third Winchester. The battle was the bloodiest in valley history. More than 9,000 soldiers died during the fight.

After the battle, Sheridan and his troops marched through the area. Carrying out a scorched-earth policy, they destroyed crops, burned homes, and killed livestock throughout the valley. People who lived there were forced to scavenge for food and take shelter in burned-out buildings. Sheridan became a much-hated man in the area.

CONFEDERATE GENERAL STONEWALL JACKSON

When the Civil War broke out in 1861, Thomas Jonathan Jackson was a professor at the Virginia Military Institute in the Shenandoah Valley. Called Tom Fool by his students, Jackson earned another, more lasting nickname early in the Civil War. During the Battle of First Manassas, Jackson was said to have stood as firm in battle as a stone wall. Robert E. Lee, commander of the Confederate army, considered Stonewall Jackson his finest commander. Jackson was killed during the Battle of Chancellorsville, shot accidentally by his own men.

Union forces of Benson's Battery in the Battle of Seven Pines stand guard in the fighting against General Thomas "Stonewall" Jackson's Confederate troops at Fair Oaks near Richmond, Virginia.

The Shenandoah Area Today

A horse grazes amid farm silos in the Shenandoah Mountains in western Rockingham County near Harrisonburg, Virginia.

Over the years, increased development and industry in the Shenandoah area have threatened the health of the Shenandoah River. Fertilizers, mercury, and other chemicals have seeped or been dumped into the river, polluting the water and contaminating the fish. People concerned about the river's health have formed groups and pushed for legislation to clean up the Shenandoah. Today, the river is healthier than it was a few decades ago.

Tourism

The Shenandoah River and Valley are tourist attractions filled with natural beauty as well as history. Visitors to the Shenandoah River can enjoy tubing, whitewater rafting, kayaking, and canoeing. The river is also a well-known fishing site stocked with bass and other fish. Another area attraction is Shenandoah National Park and Skyline Drive, a scenic road through the Blue Mountains.

Each year, the chance to tread in the footsteps of Civil War soldiers attracts thousands of people to the Shenandoah Valley. In recent years, however, growth and development in the area have jeopardized many of the historic battlegrounds. Efforts are being made to preserve these important pieces of U.S. history for future generations.

The valley's unique geography draws people to the region, too. The Shenandoah's acidic groundwater and limestone soil make it the perfect environment for caves, sinkholes, natural chimneys, bridges, and arches. Luray, Virginia, is home to the Luray Caverns. Each year, half a million people visit these famous caves. One of the highlights of the caverns is an organ that was fashioned out of *stalactites*, icicle-shaped formations that hang from the roofs of caves. Created in 1954 by Leland Sprinkle, the organ can actually be played.

FAMOUS VALLEY FOLK

Woodrow Wilson—The twenty-eighth president of the United States was born in Staunton, Virginia, in 1856. World War I (1914–1918) began during Wilson's presidency.

Patsy Cline—The famous country singer, born in Winchester in 1933, recorded the songs "Crazy," "Sweet Dreams," and "Walking After Midnight."

WILLA CATHER

Willa Cather—Although born in Winchester, Virginia, in 1873, Cather is best known for her novels about prairie life. The Pulitzer Prize–winning author wrote *O Pioneers!* and *My Antonia.*

Sources

BOOKS

Boles, John B. *The South through Time: A History of an American Region.* Englewood Cliffs, NJ: Prentice Hall, 1995.

Doherty, Kieran. *Soldiers, Cavaliers, and Planters: Settlers of the Southeastern Colonies.* Minneapolis: Oliver Press, 1999.

Dubowski, Cathy East. *Clara Barton: Healing the Wounds.* Englewood Cliffs, NJ: Silver Burdett Press, Inc., 1991.

Dubowski, Cathy East. *Robert E. Lee and the Rise of the South.* Englewood Cliffs, NJ: Silver Burdett Press, Inc., 1991.

Hakim, Joy. *Reconstruction and Reform.* New York: Oxford University Press, 1994.

Reger, James P. *Life in the South During the Civil War.* San Diego: Lucent Books, 1997.

WEB SITES

American Rivers *www.amrivers.org*

Civilwar.com *www.civilwar.com*

The Civil War Home Page *www.civil-war.net*

Florida Keys History Museum *www.keyshistory.org*

Mine Safety and Health Administration *www.msha.gov*

North American Association for Environmental Education—EE Link: Southeast Region *eelink.net/region-southeast.html*

U.S. Census Bureau: American FactFinder *factfinder.census.gov/servlet/BasicFactsServlet*

Virginia's Indians, Past and Present *falcon.jmu.edu/~ramseyil/vaindians.htm*

Index